The
SECRET GARDENS
of
CHARLESTON

The
SECRET GARDENS
of
CHARLESTON

LOUISA PRINGLE CAMERON

Principal Photography by Lauren Preller Chambers

➤

Wyrick & Company

Charleston

First Edition
09 08 07 06 05 5 4 3 2 1

Published by
Wyrick & Company
An imprint of Gibbs Smith, Publisher
P.O. Box 667
Layton, Utah 84041

Orders: 1.800.748.5439
www.gibbs-smith.com

Designed by Sandra Strother Hudson
Printed and bound in China

Library of Congress Cataloging-in-Publication Data

Cameron, Louisa Pringle, 1953-
[Charleston gardener]
The secret gardens of Charleston / Louisa Pringle Cameron ;
principal photography by Lauren Preller Chambers.
p. cm
Orginally published as: Charleston gardener, c2001.
ISBN 0-941711-78-1
1. Gardens—South Carolina—Charleston. 2. Gardens—South
Carolina—Charleston—Pictorial works. 3. Charleston (S.C.)—
Description and travel. I. Chambers, Lauren Preller, 1956- II. Title

SB466.U65C532 2005
712'.6'09757915—dc22

                              2005044348

THIS BOOK IS DEDICATED WITH LOVE TO MY SISTER

ANNE BUIST PRINGLE SNOWDEN

Contents

Preface

Charleston, founded in 1670, has an important history of gardening. It has been as alluring to horticulturists as it has been appealing to sophisticated travelers throughout its history. Mark Catesby, a naturalist, historian, and artist, documented plants and sent them (along with seeds) back to England in the early 1700s. The French government funded André Michaux's plant collecting expeditions to America, where he and his son eventually established a nursery near Charleston in 1787. The Gardenia and the Poinsettia were named for botanically-minded early Charlestonians, and the first rose to be hybridized in America, Champneys' Pink Cluster, was grown at a large garden just south of the city.

Today, thousands of visitors make spring pilgrimages to see the trio of famous plantation gardens near Charleston: Cypress Gardens, Magnolia Gardens, and Middleton Place. The architecture and the gardens of the city are beautiful all year long, and the Historic Charleston Foundation and the Preservation Society sponsor private house and garden tours in the spring and fall, respectively. Because of the generosity of the homeowners, visitors are able to see the intimate walled courtyards and gardens of the old city at their best during these special times of year.

The climate here is generally balmy, but is quite hot and humid in the summer. The average growing season is about 294 days, with December 10th as the average date of first frost and February 19th the last. The average annual rainfall is 48 inches. Our USDA planting zone is frequently listed as Zone 8, but is considered by many to be Zone 9 near the water and in protected micro-climates. Heat tolerance needs to be taken into account as well as cold tolerance.

On the night of September 21, 1989, Hurricane Hugo slammed into Charleston harbor and churned across the city. Wind speeds reached 138 m.p.h. at a Coast Guard buoy tender in Yellowhouse Creek off the Cooper River. The storm tide measured at Romain Retreat at the southern end of Bull's Bay about 40 miles north of Charleston was the highest recorded anywhere on the East Coast of the United States in this century, according to data supplied by the U. S. Weather Service at Charleston International Airport. During a hurricane in 1893, the storm tide was 8.15 feet above mean sea level downtown. For Hurricane Hugo it was 10.4 feet. From approximately 9:00 p.m. until midnight, when the eye of the storm passed over, the hurricane raged. A few hours later, a stunned populace was left to deal with the destruction while the storm itself continued northwest over the Carolinas, the Virginias, Pennsylvania, and on to the Canadian border.

In October 1989, I wrote a letter to the editors of *House and Garden* magazine, enclosing some pictures of our property after the storm. They had sent Mick Hales to Charleston to photograph gardens in July of 1989 and ours had been included. The article was never published. In my letter was an account of the storm and its aftermath that expressed the feelings of so many of us: grief-stricken, confused, grateful to be alive, and yet ready to move ahead. I wrote:

> Eighty percent of the roofs were damaged and at least two-thirds of the trees, especially the big ones, were down. The churches were particularly hard-hit. As we picked our way through the mud and around the debris, we saw gardens full of salt water, chimneys toppled, front doors blown in, walls in pieces . . . and the bridge across the inland waterway to the islands sticking straight up out of the water. . . .
>
> As I write, the tree crews are in the middle of their fourth day of getting our trees off of our fences and our neighbors' property. But not only will we replant, we will completely overhaul the back garden. Price can't wait to investigate pond options. . . . I actually was glad to lose a ratty-looking magnolia and two hackberry trees, but we are all sorry for the loss of the big oak and the elms. We may plant crab apples for a screen from the school to the south. We have lots of sun now.

I had started writing my first book, *The Private Gardens of Charleston,* in May 1989, and decided to finish it without dwelling on the storm. It was an emotional topic and everyone was still dealing with contractors, roofers, insurance companies, and stump removal in the spring of 1990. The changes which took place in many of the gardens as a result of Hurricane Hugo are given a prominent place in this sequel. However, as in the first book, the real story is of the gardeners themselves, a remarkable group of talented, generous, and indomitably-spirited people.

While many of the gardens have similar plant material and some even have similar plats and hardscapes, each one is highly individual and reflects its owners' tastes and talents. For those beginning a garden or wishing to re-establish one, I hope these will be an inspiration. To me they are an absolute joy.

Acknowledgements

As with most books, there are always people behind the scenes lending support and providing encouragement. My family has been wonderful, but again, the credit goes to the gardeners themselves—an intrepid and generous group of talented and hard workers.

Lauren Preller Chambers, who provided most of the photographs, was a delight to work with and was always willing to run back to get just the right shots. Charles Cornwell, my editor, had a keen eye for detail, and Dianne Avlon generously gave of her time to proofread.

But a tremendous and heartfelt thank you goes to my publisher, Pete Wyrick. He gently insisted that I finally learn to type and to use a computer (the manuscript for my first book was hand-written), and patiently waited for the result—a manuscript on a floppy disk! Thank you, Pete, it's been a lot of fun.

The
SECRET GARDENS
of
CHARLESTON

A Garden in Ansonborough

In his informative recent book *The Buildings of Charleston,* Jonathan H. Poston describes Ansonborough as Charleston's first suburb: "By the eighteenth century this borough was home to various merchants, relatively prosperous tradesmen, and even a few planters." The wealthy merchant Henry Laurens, who was also a president of the Continental Congress, owned four acres at the northern edge of Ansonborough and brought an English gardener to the city in 1767. On this acreage grew "olives, capers, limes, ginger, guinea grass, Alpine strawberries, raspberries, grapes, apples, pears, and plums, in addition to many flowering shrubs and herbs."

"[In] 1838, a fire broke out...that [proved] to be 'the largest and most distressing fire' in the city to that date." By the 1850s, Mr. Poston continues, whole rows of mostly brick houses had been newly constructed. By World War II, however, the neighborhood had gone into a "significant decline." It was subsequently "targeted by Historic Charleston Foundation in 1958 as its first revolving fund enterprise, the Ansonborough Rehabilitation Project."

Burton White, a retired maritime lawyer from New York, moved to Charleston in the 1970s, and in 1972 he built a modern house in Ansonborough with a facade sympathetic to the surrounding architecture. The garden, however, was a little unusual. Mr. White had enjoyed having a Japanese style garden at his home in Brooklyn, so he had a plan drawn by a designer in Japan that would fit the dimensions of the area behind his new house in Charleston, to be viewed from glass walls on both storeys. The garden from the street entrance was designed to be somewhat European and featured four Italian cypresses punctuating a short walkway "vista" between two C-shaped flowerbeds surrounded by holly (*Ilex vomitoria*) hedges.

The present owners moved to the property in 1990, three months after Hurricane Hugo. Two of the cypresses had been destroyed, an enormous elm tree to the east had been badly beaten, and the gate to the Japanese garden had been torn off its hinges and accidentally thrown out with other storm debris. The house, built on a slab and made of pre-stressed concrete, withstood the storm with very little damage.

The new owners got to work right away. Both of them gardeners keen on design, they decided to keep the basic plans of the gardens that were Mr. Burton's legacy. Fortunately, they had a copy of the design for the Japanese gate and had it replicated. Two Italian cypresses were purchased to take the place of the storm victims and the

FACING PAGE: *The Japanese garden.*

2

Italian cypresses dominate the front garden.

family was "astounded" that the replacements quickly caught up with the established pair. The consulting arborist for the garden thinks that the trees, now over forty feet in height, are some of the tallest of their variety in the city.

The flowerbeds all needed refurbishing. The formal holly beds are in full sun and now contain a whimsical selection of vegetables and salad greens instead of late-blooming Gumpo azaleas. Interesting old and modern sculpture complements banana shrub *(Michelia Wgo)*, camellias, anise *(Illicium floridanum)*, Japanese plum *(Eriobotrya japonica)*, and a formal planting of Greek myrtle *(Myrtus communis)*. Other blooming plants include old-fashioned stock, delphiniums, snapdragons, yarrow, ranunculus, iris, and Japanese anemones.

The Japanese garden has a stone "frozen river streambed" which encircles a miniature island and is built on a slope so that when it rains, it comes alive. A narrow path, shaded by maples, leads around the periphery and crosses a bridge. Several delicate fountains are tucked in among a variety of oriental plant material particularly suited to the southern climate. Bamboo, nandina (heavenly bamboo), aucuba, camellias, ferns, junipers, and a bonsai form of cedar all grow well in the shade. Mondo grass *(Ophiopogon japonicus)* imitates windblown grasses along the edge of the stream.

Reflecting on their two gardens, the present owner's wife agrees with her husband's observation: "We go from East to West and from the sacred to the profane."

LEFT: *A mural painted by the owners' daughter decorates the upstairs porch.* RIGHT: *One of the garden's sculptures.*

A Garden in the Crescent

Records from 1853 show a plantation just to the west of Charleston called The Crescent, named for its location on the crescent-shaped acreage between the Ashley River and the mouth of the Stono River. In 1926, the property was divided for development, and the firm of Frederick Law Olmsted was hired to draw up the site plans.

Mr. and Mrs. John MacDougal moved to the Crescent in 1969, into a white brick house built in 1936 on a lot that measures a little over an acre. Mrs. MacDougal, a native of upstate New York, has been a gardener all of her life and is a woman of many talents, which she generously shares with the community. In addition to her former credentials as a New York State horticulture judge and a National Council of Flower Shows judge, she published a pamphlet for the Historic Charleston Foundation on the most common flowers seen blooming seasonally in the city of Charleston. She is a licensed City Guide and a flower arranger, a passion which she has turned into an art form for a few special clients.

A walk through Mrs. MacDougal's garden any time of year is not only a delight to the senses, but also quite an education. To screen out traffic noises, provide privacy, and give a tall, dark green background for plantings, a ligustrum hedge and other screening shrubs were planted around the property on three sides. On the fourth side, the house faces a lawn which stretches away into the marshy edges of the river. There are deep flowerbeds all around the house and along the perimeter. Many of the flowering shrubs are reached by paths that wind through mature azaleas and camellias. Also in the background are *Illicium anisatum*, *Viburnum tinus*, *Spiraea prunifolia* (bridal wreath), 'Anthony Waterer' spiraea, *Spiraea reevesiana*, *Callicarpa americana* (beautyberry), and *Gordonia*. Some of the paths are paved, while others are subtly marked with a bit of whimsy, such as Virginia Metalcrafters' giant leaves. Near the house a "grandchildren's" garden of miniature plants, seating, and sculpture is hidden within thick bushes. Berms of salt-tolerant plants have been placed near the edge of the marsh and pots line the driveway, steps, back terrace, and porch.

"While a master plan is grand, and I heartily approve of one, I don't have any plan," explains Mrs. MacDougal. "I usually see a plant, buy it, and then figure out where to plant it," she laughs. "I am a patient person and enjoy taking cuttings and planting from seed." She also enjoys a challenge. In the 1970s, she was intrigued by the limited number of daffodils (which are all technically members of the narcissus

FACING PAGE: *An early morning view of the brick steps leading down to the marsh.*

The "mume allée" of flowering apricots. FACING PAGE: *Mrs. MacDougal, framed by* Loropetalum, *in her garden.*

family) that were grown by local gardeners and began buying many bulbs and keeping detailed records. Each year, she orders several varieties of bulbs and plants them in groups of ten, carefully labeled. Data are compiled on the computer and show initial bloom, peak bloom, hardiness, repeat bloom, color, etc. Starting in January with the yellow cup paper whites, there is a succession of bloom which lasts through the end of April and which includes dozens of varieties. Each year at the fall Garden Festival, a charitable fundraiser, Mrs. MacDougal volunteers to lend her considerable expertise by manning a booth selling the bulbs which she hand selects and packages.

The trial garden for her bulbs is in an allée of *Prunus Mume*, the Japanese flowering apricot, located along the east side of the house. Each of the eight trees is a separate variety with a slightly different pink blossom, ranging from nearly white to nearly red. Other oriental flowering trees she has in the garden are *Prunus subhirtella* 'Autumnalis', *P. campanulata* (Taiwan cherry), *P. Persica* (flowering peach), *P. serrulata* 'Kwanzan', *P. yedoensis* (Yoshino cherry), *Cornus Kousa* (dogwood), and an orange-flowering tea olive she first saw in Japan.

Collecting and successfully growing unusual plants is one of Mrs. MacDougal's favorite pastimes. "If it's been on the cover of the Park Seed or the Wayside Gardens catalog, I've probably tried it," she admits. A few of the less familiar plants she cultivates are *Exochorda* (pearlbush), several native azaleas and a small-flowered lavender azalea said to be Mr. E. I. duPont's favorite, *Choisya* (Mexican rose, which is tender here, but has fragrant blooms in winter), a *Cestrum Parqui* (willow-leaved jessamine) from Penelope Hobhouse, *Amsonia*, a few grevilleas that are native to Australia, which she has planted in the inhospitable environment of live oak tree roots, *Neolitsea*, a somewhat rare deep orange *Lilium pumilum*, and *Clytostoma*, a vine that resembles a "big purple bignonia" to Mrs. MacDougal. The ability to recognize the cotyledons of numerous plants is useful to someone who describes herself as a "flinger of seeds." " I move plants around frequently, too, always trying for the best spot for the specimen."

Mrs. MacDougal grows plants specifically with flower arranging in mind. Loropetalum, spiraea, wisteria, larkspur, honeysuckle, quince, mock orange *(Philadelphus)*, daylilies, hydrangeas, cannas, oriental poppies, privet, sea myrtle *(Baccharis halimifolia)*, tea olive, amaryllis, yarrow, fothergilla, cosmos, and daisies can be seen in her bouquets. "Daffodils release carbon dioxide, which is toxic to other flowers, for at least an hour after cutting and need to be separated for that hour before adding them to an arrangement," she informs. There are over sixty camellias under the shade of live oaks in the garden, which give a breathtaking display. Mrs.

A Charleston "joggling board" awaits young visitors.

MacDougal's favorite is the pink 'Catherine Cathcart.' There is also a mature *Magnolia grandiflora* next to the house and its branches sweep the lawn.

The family left the premises during Hurricane Hugo in 1989 and it took over two hours with a chainsaw to get back into the driveway. "We did all of the gardening ourselves before the storm, but now I need help. Hugo altered the climate of the gardens here by changing the shade/sun ratio and thus raising the soil temperature," she explains. "Temperatures as little as a degree higher can allow certain weed seeds to finally germinate. I have wild cannas that exploded out of the ground the summer after the storm."

For an avid gardener like Mrs. MacDougal, the garden is always in a state of flux, but that is the way she prefers it. Her favorite gardening book is Mirabel Osler's *A Gentle Plea for Chaos*, and her philosophy is summed up by the Japanese concept "My garden is becoming. . . ."

The Garden of the Isaac Motte Dart House

When Dr. and Mrs. E. G. Johnson III purchased this large uptown property, they were prepared for the challenge of a major restoration and worked closely with the Historic Charleston Foundation to protect the lot and its buildings for the future. The house sits on about an acre and has a notable early Gothic Revival brick carriage house that was built toward the back of the lot. The two-and-a-half-storeyed main house is wooden and sits on a high brick basement facing the street. It was originally a "single" house, but a nineteenth-century rear addition altered its floor plan to that of a double house (i.e., four rooms on each floor divided by a central hall.) This addition was so badly damaged by Hurricane Hugo in 1989 that it was torn down after the storm. After the Johnsons bought the property in 1994, they renovated and occupied the carriage house until the main house was finished and another rear addition was constructed.

As for the garden, there was none. For decades the house and its dependency had been used as a school and dormitory. Except for one small, weedy plot, the entire area was a black asphalt parking lot complete with concrete tire stops and numbered spaces. A six-inch-thick regulation concrete sidewalk extended all the way along the side of both buildings through the property.

With the help of his sons, Dr. Johnson began the laborious task of digging up and removing the paving, which was carted off in several loads. Cobblestones, which formed earlier paving, were discovered underneath the asphalt and also had to be excavated. The next step was to remove the chainlink fence and redefine the property lines with wooden fencing (to be eventually replaced with brick walls). More than thirty loads of Johns Island topsoil and compost from the Bee's Ferry landfill were spread over the area in preparation for outlining the beds and borders. Because the carriage house sits four feet higher and fifty feet away from the main house, the landscape had to be professionally graded.

"It was daunting to be faced with a blank slate," remembers Dr. Johnson. "There were only two trees on the property after the storm: a tall palmetto and a Darlington oak that is said to be the largest survivor in the city. It was probably planted about the time the house was built." Dr. Johnson has always enjoyed gardening and decided to try his hand at landscape design. He sketched the general layout for a driveway, a parking court, walkways, a formal entrance, and a series of six separate gardens laid out along the main axes of the property.

FACING PAGE: *Western view from an upstairs window in the carriage house. A Darlington oak is to the right.*

The first installation was a formal parterre garden in front of the carriage house. Four raised brick beds planted with St. Augustine grass and bordered with 'Beckett's' boxwoods surround a circular bed in the middle, which is planted annually. Hollies were planted along the north and west borders for privacy, including a line of fourteen Palatka holly (*Ilex x attenuata* 'East Palatka') trees. This holly, according to Michael Dirr, was discovered in the wild in Florida in 1927.

An herb garden soon developed in the sheltered area between the two houses, which are connected by a "wonderfully irregular" ten-foot, soft orange brick wall to the east. Loosely based on a design from a book on herbs, the pattern is three squares filled with diamond-shaped beds and raised planters. Two sandstone caps remained from brick pillars of the fence that used to be in front of the house, and these were arranged as part of the design.

Most of the plants used in the initial layout came from local nurseries, but a great many plants, mulch and other materials were purchased from large retail hardware and garden centers. Shell sand was the first material used for all the paths and for the car park, but its color looked too pale. It was also tracked into the houses and cars,

Noisette roses form the centerpiece of the rose garden.

and cats *loved* it. Dark gray crushed slag turned out to be a wiser choice. A number of old bricks scattered around the property were soon used to make borders, but hundreds more were needed and were purchased locally. Derek Wade, a landscaper, installed a lighting system and now helps with maintenance.

The driveway traverses the property from south to north and is lined on the east with a row of crape myrtle trees. Dividing the garden from east to west is a five-foot scalloped wooden fence, which also serves to define the garden space "belonging" to the carriage house. Between this fence and the main house is a rose and shrub garden shaped roughly like a camellia leaf. Opposite the roses and along the western length of the garden are three distinct areas with different types of planting.

The northernmost area is oriental in feel. It lies in the shade of the enormous Darlington oak tree and features a flagstone path that loops through plantings of ligustrum, ivy, fatsia, aucuba, anise, mahonia, giant liriope, and ferns. Accent trees include a dwarf maple, a weeping willow, and a vitex. Just to the right is a parking court by the gated rear entrance to the property. The Johnsons found a pair of

wrought iron gates salvaged from a cemetery in Pennsylvania with a quatrefoil de-sign similar to that of the windows in the Gothic-style carriage house. Dr. Johnson repeated the quatrefoil pattern in a pair of parterres flanking the knot garden at the southwest corner of the property. Between the oak tree and this knot garden is an arbor with a bench overlooking a sunny perennial garden that sometimes includes a few vegetables.

The Johnsons are planning to plant more trees and shrubs to add texture, depth, and contrast as the garden matures. Mrs. Johnson particularly enjoys choosing a va-riety of containers and filling them with flower combinations that enhance the different areas of the garden, but both husband and wife find gardening and the study of gardening a delightful pastime and a talent they enjoy sharing with friends.

Formal parterre garden of the gothic style carriage house.

The Garden of the John Fullerton House

Astunning example of pre-Revolutionary architecture, the John Fullerton house was constructed in 1772 by a Scottish carpenter and joiner. The two-storeyed piazza was added around 1800 and there was a Victorian addition in the late 1800s. Although formality suits the design of many of the narrow and enclosed gardens in the historic district, especially those of very grand houses, it was not until 1985 that the garden was laid out in a highly structured format.

The garden was one of landscape architect Hugh Dargan's first major projects in the city of Charleston. There were five separate areas: a paved driveway lined with lights recessed in stone markers; an oval lawn surrounded by azaleas along the south piazza; a swimming pool set behind a latticed brick privacy wall; a patio overlooking the pool; and a shady boxwood parterre garden. The parterre garden was planted at the back of the property beyond the original kitchen, a charming detached wooden building.

The current owners, Mr. and Mrs. Eric Friberg, purchased the property in the summer of 1989, just a few months before Hurricane Hugo. The storm surge flooded the lot with several feet of water, resulting in some salt kill, but the "bones" of the garden survived, including an unusually old and large cassina tree *(Ilex Cassine L.)* prized by all the owners of the property. Also surviving were a number of crape myrtles, which are colorful in the summer and fall.

Mrs. Friberg has continued the tradition of adding significant architectural elements to the house by designing a classical wooden gate and fence along the street. Almost three years in the planning and execution, the elaborate composite design is her own, derived from studies of extant as well as demolished examples in the city. Although Mrs. Donna Cox, a local landscape designer, oversees the maintenance of the garden, Mrs. Friberg takes a keen interest in the plant material and ornamentation. She has added raised planters full of blooming annuals and perennials near the pool, replaced a fountain, and added benches in the parterre garden.

The children particularly enjoy the pool. There is always a cool breeze on the piazza, even in hot weather, so breakfast and lunch are frequently taken on the lower porch in the shade of the corner overlooking the garden. The second storey of the piazza is "my tree house in the summer," says Mrs. Friberg, but her favorite time of year in her garden is the fall, when the crape myrtle leaves have begun to turn fiery, the dogwood leaves take on a burgundy cast, and the jewel-like berries of the cassina holly are ripening.

FACING PAGE, TOP: *The sculptural trunks of crape myrtles contrast with the quiet stillness of the formal garden.*
FACING PAGE, BOTTOM: *The crape myrtles begin their summer bloom.*

A Garden on Greenhill Street

One of the reasons the Schindlers were intrigued by the tiny, nineteenth-century house they now inhabit was its history of ownership. E. deMay Smith, a well-known local watercolor artist, had lived there previously and her son had designed and executed the pair of copper window boxes near the front door. Both Mrs. Schindler and her daughter are artists, and they fell in love with the charming neighborhood, a hodgepodge of small houses on a street too narrow for parking.

Mrs. Schindler, the gardener in the family, was enthusiastic about creating a flower garden that would complement the house and was excited by the idea of trying to make it look artistic, like an impressionist painting. She decided to delete the existing arrangement and start from scratch, beginning with one small area at a time. "I have no formal training," she explains, "but I was not afraid to try planting my own garden, and approaching it bit by bit worked pretty well." She went on garden tours and took notes on what thrived in the city, the time of year when plants bloomed, and what was available. The local nurserymen were particularly helpful with suggestions.

There were three small areas that could be planted: the mostly sunny front yard with an eastern exposure, a very shady north side with a patio, and a walled-in space on the west just the length of the sitting room next to it and just wide enough for a table and a chair or two. Window boxes would provide opportunities for additional color displays. One of Mrs. Schindler's hobbies is studying and collecting folk art, so adding bric-a-brac, sculpture, and assorted found objects to the garden was a great deal of fun and created interest.

"I was excited about growing flowers," says Mrs. Schindler. "Our family had been living in Connecticut on two acres overrun by a herd of deer. They ate our hostas, daylilies, tulips, and roses. I never saw a hosta even bloom on our property. So in Charleston, I just planted *everything*."

Today, the garden has something in bloom all year-round: roses and sasanquas at Christmas; pansies and snaps in winter; jasmine, bulbs, and alyssum in the spring; geraniums, phlox, petunias, and impatiens in summer. Window boxes spill periwinkle, violas, verbenas, and ferns. There are miniature cottages for the birds as well as a fishpond for them to splash in and play. It paints a lovely picture.

FACING PAGE, TOP: *Confederate jasmine spills over the mailbox and petunias bloom gaily in their windowboxes on Greenhill Street.* FACING PAGE, BOTTOM: *A riot of color in the tiny front entrance garden.*

The Garden of the Harth-Middleton House

Hurricane Hugo destroyed most of the trees in the large garden attached to the Harth-Middleton House (circa 1800), which is located near Charleston's famous waterfront promenade, the Battery. Along the walled perimeter of the garden, an assortment of evergreens, including pines, magnolias, live oaks, and hollies, had formerly surrounded a sloping lawn. A bright blue kidney-shaped pool next to the house looked forlorn and somewhat out of style. Neighboring houses were now in plain view. Privacy, or at least the illusion of it, was no more.

The house, which had undergone major renovations after the earthquake of 1886, was extensively renovated again in the 1920s and the landscape architect Loutrel Briggs laid out a formal garden to the west of the building. The present owners, the Pelzers, bought the house in the 1970s.

After the hurricane, the Pelzers decided to completely redo the landscape. Realizing that the Briggs plan could not be resurrected, the Pelzers consulted local landscape architect T. Hunter McEaddy. Mr. Pelzer had always liked the terraces, water, and different levels frequently seen in Italian gardens and asked that the design be loosely based on those features. The end result has a wonderful European appearance with a sense of the American semitropical South.

Before the yard was redesigned, a balcony that ran along the west facade of the house was removed and replaced with a raised terrace overlooking the pool. Accessible from the house through glass doors and from the garden by a paved staircase, the terrace solved the problem of a lack of connection between the house and garden and provided an elevated view of the longitudinal main vista, a fountain beyond an oval lawn.

Within the irregular rectangle of the lot, McEaddy drew a cruciform design, emphasizing a natural slope from the east, where an old seawall had been covered with a large berm to raise the area for a pool by the house. The owners wanted to keep the swimming pool, so Mr. McEaddy surrounded it with brick paving and a dwarf yaupon holly hedge and incorporated it into the plan for a series of level changes. Stone steps leading from the pool enter the north-south axis of the garden, a paved court between grassy rectangles, with a gate to the street at the southern end and a fanciful "temple" to the north. Urns on pedestals and Italian cypresses symmetrically punctuate the walks. Eight majestic Canary Island date palms (*Phoenix canariensis*) tower above.

FACING PAGE: *Parterres filled with roses flank a fountain at the far end of the garden.*

22

At the far west wall of the garden, huge southern magnolias *(Magnolia grandiflora)* provide an evergreen background and an effective privacy screen from other houses, suggesting the feeling of being out in the country. Four-foot high glossy leaf privet hedges *(Ligustrum japonicum)* section off this end of the garden, which features a water jet fountain. The fountain has wide raised edges on its shallow pool and all the mechanisms are recessed, making it available to the children, who love to run across the thick, grassy oval lawn and up and down the steps back and forth from the pool into the fountain.

Liriope, a vigorous member of the lily family, covers the ground under an allée of crape myrtles.

Privacy is usually a priority in city gardens, particularly from the street. A false yew hedge (*Podocarpus macrophyllus*), which tolerates heavy shade, grows along the wrought iron fence along the sidewalk, under the live oaks. As one comes in from the street gate, one sees an oval court that anchors the entrance to the terrace and to a small allée of five pairs of crape myrtles. The variety of myrtle (*Lagerstroemia indica* 'Natchez') was chosen for its white blossoms and deep cinnamon-colored peeling bark. Dwarf mondo grass, which does not need much light or soil and tends not to catch the foot, is planted between square paving stones beneath the trees.

The original plan included a pergola over the grass walk along the northern border of the formal garden, but the rapid growth of the magnolias planted against the wall that defines the property line may have effectively precluded the need for a structural screen. Closer to the house, on the same northern boundary, a small water garden was installed. This area has a subtropical looseness and overgrown look, in contrast to the formality of the main garden, and is particularly enjoyed by the young children in the family.

The project was successful, not only in terms of transforming the landscape, but also in terms of awakening and stimulating Mr. Pelzer's personal interest in hands-on work in the garden. According to Mr. McEaddy, he is his only client who became a passionate gardener after the installation instead of starting out as a gardener in the first place.

The Formal Garden
of the Andrew Hasell House

Built in 1789, the Andrew Hasell house was purchased in this century by Mr. and Mrs. Thomas Huguenin, parents of the present owner. The Huguenins restored the house in the 1930s and established a small formal garden, behind which, recalls Mrs. Richard E. Coen, "Papa used to keep turkeys, Muscovy ducks, and lots of dogs." A dense stand of bamboo screened the back of the deep lot where a garage—a luxury in the city—was later constructed, as off-street parking used to be required at night by city ordinance. The garage was accessible only via a narrow lane along the house, so the family's automobile had to be selected according to the width of the vehicle. The Huguenins' solution was to make a gift of the lane to the city (which purchased three additional feet to widen the access) in exchange for off-street garbage collection.

Bright spring annuals emphasize the unusual horseshoe shape of a flowerbed.

The original sketch for the existing garden was made for the Huguenins by the late

Mary Mikell Barnwell, who worked with Loutrel Briggs, a well-known local architect. Mrs. Barnwell designed curved brick walls to enclose the yard and created flowerbeds in unusual shapes. Two lawns, divided by a terrace, end in a horseshoe-shaped bed featuring a small statue and colorful displays of annuals. The thirty-four-by-twelve-foot "chair" bed mimics the pattern of the back of an old chair on display in the Charleston Museum's Heyward-Washington House, whose stately Georgian facade can be seen directly beyond the garden.

In 1964, the Coens moved into the house and slowly began making the changes that would become their signature. A major renovation of the house has just been completed. During the 1960s, refurbishment of the garden was done in sections. Pittosporum and ligustrum hedges, which had grown tall and leggy, were removed entirely and replaced with more slowly growing podocarpus and 'Kingsville' boxwood. An enormous old wisteria vine was untangled and destroyed; it had worked its way into a wall and had loosened the bricks.

Low brick borders were added to outline the house and small lawn, and flowerbeds were widened to extend planting against the high walls. Several enormous flagstones were brought in to pave a terrace for outdoor dining, and blooming shrubs were set in new locations. Simms McDowell, Sr. had inspired Mr. Coen to grow camellias and gave advice on the choice of the specimens which remain in the garden today.

"There are several amusing stories about the garden," relates Mrs. Coen, adding that one of her favorites is about her husband's approach to plant husbandry. "He had been working all day and asked me to come see what had been accomplished. I told him that the garden looked just great, but he wanted to know if I had noticed just exactly what had been done. Well, I repeated hedgingly, you've been working hard and it shows. I was still clueless. Then he proudly pointed out that he had moved each one of the half-dozen boxwood shrubs on the north side of the lawn to the south side (and vice versa) to balance their sun exposure and improve their growth. Not a piece of mulch was out of place!"

Visitors frequently remark on the stylish formality of the garden, with its immaculate grooming and its careful choice and placement of plants. The house, also formal, embraces the garden on its southern aspect. An elliptical lawn, surrounded by tightly clipped shrubs and small trees, extends along the two-storeyed porch of the house, narrows at one end, and leads onto the terrace. A second lawn, this one enclosed by low boxwoods, separates the terrace from the "horseshoe" and "chair" beds. Azaleas and bedding plants make the garden particularly showy in the spring. Much thought and attention have been given to color, design, and scale throughout.

Hurricane Hugo struck exactly twenty-five years after the Coens moved into the house. Fortunately, three months before the storm, an arborist had trimmed the

*The pink and white blossoms
of impatiens and crape myrtle
emphasize the soft rich hues
of Charleston brick.*

FACING PAGE: *The
distinctively patterned "chair"
bed at the Andrew Hasell
house.*

large crape myrtle and magnolia trees, pruned the weight out of their interiors, and
fertilized them. Luckily, they survived the hurricane. After the storm, an irrigation
system, outdoor lighting, and ironwork supports for fragrant Confederate jasmine
vines were installed against two tall walls to give more interest. The "moonlighting"
turned out to be an especially wonderful addition, lending a candlelight atmosphere
perfect for al fresco entertaining and evening strolls. Yet another project has been the
reworking and landscaping of the parking area, which will give the Coens just that
little bit more planting space all gardeners crave.

The Hannah Heyward House Garden

Prominently situated on one of the city's loveliest residential streets is a handsome Georgian clapboard house. It was built in 1789 by Mrs. William Heyward, the sister-in-law of Thomas Heyward, signer of the Declaration of Independence. Since the 1860s, the property has remained in the same family, which has a tradition of gardening as well as stewardship.

A central hall running through the house opens onto a garden of about half an acre, considered a generous size in the old part of the city. Totally enclosed by brick walls, the garden contains large groupings of traditional camellias, azaleas, and sasanquas, a formal terrace, charming kitchen buildings, a stable and a vegetable plot. A greenhouse supplies plants for the conservatory, which is an enclosed porch on the south side of the house.

The owner's mother, Mrs. Augustine Smythe, had Loutrel Briggs install a design that included a lawn with a gentle descent down wide, curving brick stairs to a flagstone terrace, a trellised arch, holly and false yew hedges, and a boxwood circle as a focal point. The bones of this design remain, but the present Mrs. Smythe has imprinted the garden with her personality. There used to be a clay tennis court at the far end of the property, but it was several feet short of a regulation court. When the children grew up and left home, she removed the court, which is now the site of a greenhouse as well as a vegetable, a cutting and a rose garden. She grew up on a nine-acre garden in Bermuda that also had a greenhouse and a conservatory. Her mother, an international flower arranger, was flown to London by the Bermudians to make an arrangement in Westminster Abbey using the flowers of their country during the celebration of Empire Day. Not surprisingly, Mrs. Smythe also loves to arrange flowers and has done so for many years for Saint Michael's Episcopal Church.

While the Charleston climate is too harsh for outdoor planting of the tender tropicals of Bermuda, Mrs. Smythe does grow clivias, bougainvilleas, plumerias (frangipane), and philodendrons in the conservatory. Hibiscus, grown in large planters, goes into the greenhouse in winter. A fascinating bromeliad, inherited from Mr. Smythe's mother, is called Queen's-Tears and produces stems with navy blue and yellow-striped clusters of blooms.

Some of the oldest specimens in the garden are the trees. There are several huge crape myrtles (*Lagerstroemia*) and live oaks (*Quercus virginiana*). A China Fir fruit (*Cunninghamia*) dominates the north side of the house. Some old pomegranate trees continue to exhibit their exotic deep orange waxy blossoms (although they

FACING PAGE, TOP: *Azaleas are the glory of Charleston gardens in the spring.* FACING PAGE, BOTTOM: *After Hurricane Hugo, neighboring houses came into view.*

produce no fruit). A ginger collection dating back two or more generations has flourished.

Hurricane Hugo left its mark on the property in 1989. The family had to cut paths with a chainsaw afterwards. "You couldn't even get the screen doors open," recalls Mrs. Smythe. "Debris was chest high in the yard and there was no privacy screen of greenery any more. We could see a neighbor's four-poster bed on a second floor, because the corner of her house had been knocked off. We cleaned up like ants, pulling each piece of wreckage out one at a time." Most of the camellias were casualties, a huge magnolia with an unusual double trunk was downed, and eighty feet of brick wall collapsed. In addition, the barn was squashed and the conservatory badly damaged. Only the hunting dogs were unfazed by the chaos: they gleefully swam in the storm waters trapped in the back yard for three days.

The whole ecology of the garden changed, explains Mrs. Smythe. The loss of the old magnolia resulted in direct afternoon sun exposure and a whole new range of growing possibilities. A sprinkler system was installed and has been of great benefit. Each year, she orders at least a hundred more caladium bulbs to plant when the warm weather arrives. All summer long, the green, pink, red, and white variegated leaves line flowerbeds throughout the garden. In October, they are dug and put in

A vigorous climber, the Cherokee rose blooms once a year.

34

mesh bags or peach baskets and stored in the attic. The vegetable garden produces quantities of lettuce, peas, onions, cabbages, collards, and okra.

In addition to a great deal of maintenance, assisted by a hired crew, ongoing projects include installing a serpentine bed along the driveway to the outbuildings and creating a wildflower garden in the lee of a high brick wall. Here, gaillardia, verbenas, evening primroses, and other "strays from the roadside" are collected and may turn up in some of the lovely seasonal arrangements enjoyed by the parishioners of St. Michael's Church.

The Garden of the Kohne-Leslie House

Mrs. Joseph H. McGee is one of Charleston's best-known gardeners. For over twenty-five years, she perfected the art of courtyard gardening at her former address on Church Street, and is frequently sought out for advice and consultation. She entertains many celebrities of the gardening world, including visitors from abroad; and, through her involvement in organizations, she is instrumental in bringing gardening experts to Charleston for seminars and lectures.

In 1993, an exciting change occurred in her life: the McGee family moved. Their new residence, the Kohne-Leslie house, is located in the Ansonborough Historic District and was built in 1847. In the 1960s, a wooden building on the south side of the lot was removed to enlarge the garden. Landscape architect Loutrel Briggs then designed an early spring garden for the owners, who spent only the winter months in Charleston.

An immediate challenge presented itself to the McGees after the May 1993 move: one of their daughters was engaged to be married that October and the family wanted to have the reception in the house and garden. This deadline was the impetus for reorganizing the entire garden.

The house, which is several storeys tall, faces west, but its wide porches overlook the garden to the south. A brick kitchen building, used as guest quarters, sits immediately behind the house. At the far southern boundary, wrought iron gates open from the street onto a driveway which leads into a garage. In between lies the garden and a shady courtyard. The first step in Mrs. McGee's new garden design was to remove a serpentine border, take out the azaleas that constituted most of the existing shrubbery, and start planting material to screen the view of the garage, which Mrs. McGee describes as "hardly an architectural gem, but important for our needs." She also removed a yaupon holly hedge that separated the kitchen building from its courtyard and planted bay laurels. The bay laurel, which is nicknamed 'slow-as-the-mischief,' was to be the start of a kitchen garden full of herbs.

Then the real fun began. With the help of Sheila Wertimer, a local landscape architect; Beverly Rivers, a garden consultant and designer specializing in annuals and perennials; George Hyam, a local nurseryman; Jo Ann Breeland, a horticulturist with the City of Charleston; and several other gardening experts, Mrs. McGee started the installation of parterres, walks, flowerbeds, and pavement, along with the initial planting of perennials, herbs, and annuals. Shrubs, trees, and vines were carefully placed, and, as necessary, rearranged. Two fountains were also added; one

FACING PAGE, TOP: *The brick-pillared porch opens directly into the garden.*
FACING PAGE, BOTTOM: *The chartreuse leaves of sweet potato vines light up the shaded courtyard.*

directly in front of the ground floor porch leading into the garden and the other in the center of the kitchen building courtyard. A local arborist was brought in to properly prune the graceful live oak planted by Mr. Briggs in 1968, which now dominated the garden and shaded it too densely. By October the garden was just lovely for the wedding.

For Mrs. McGee, collecting unusual plants is one of the most enjoyable aspects of her hands-on approach to gardening. She travels often and usually manages to bring home a specimen or two. Arranging plants in a wide variety of containers is another one of her favorite types of gardening. Our mild winters have allowed her to experiment with tropicals and subtropicals, but many must be protected from the cold. To avoid losing valuable plants, the McGees have large platform dollies that can be rolled in and out of the garage with the potted plants placed upon them. A cold frame and a small greenhouse were installed in a work area tucked out of sight. Very large pots are accommodated in a section of the downstairs porch that is temporarily enclosed with plastic during the months when there is a danger of frost.

Autumn has always been Mrs. McGee's favorite time of year in her garden. She prunes and cuts back heavily in July for a showy fall display, then cuts back again around Thanksgiving. After the heat and humidity of summer, September, October, and November are wonderful months in the garden. Mrs. McGee remarks that at this time of year, there is a grand sense of the "Southernness of the garden, in all its lushness and heady scents." In the fall, she has a remarkable display of bananas, gingers, clerodendrums, cupheas, cestrums, solanums, and coleus spilling from pots and flowerbeds and running up and along walls, porches, and decorative supports. A firm believer in using plants which are reliable and hardy, Mrs. McGee finds that it is a "challenge to find the plants which adapt to our poor drainage, heat, and humidity," but she will occasionally nurture a few marginal specimens.

Nurturing is a large part of her *modus operandi*. With hundreds of pots and containers full of plants, Mrs. McGee spends a great deal of time watering by hand, a task she finds relaxing. Gardening is the one hobby that totally enthralls her. "This is *all* I do," she notes. " I spend a lot of time thinking about the plant world and I like for my garden to engage the viewer not just visually, but also audibly, tactually, and emotionally." A room that opens onto the porch and the garden serves as her office and library. Spilling over with books, catalogs, notes, file cabinets and baskets full of references, correspondence, and photographs, it reflects the dynamic but organized garden outside. Not surprisingly, Mrs. McGee is already making plans to revamp earlier plantings. "The back wall needs something that will stop the eye—I think a pair of loquats will do the job—and I need to have more texture and fall color over here, so I'll take out the crabapple and put in a Japanese maple . . . well, this is simply a full-time job," she smiles.

A List of Many of the Plants Found in the Garden of Mr. and Mrs. McGee

BULBS, LILIES, AND RHIZOMES

Acorus Calamus 'Variegatus'

A. gramineus 'Minimus Aureus' (dwarf golden sweet flag)

A. gramineus 'Ogon'

Agapanthus africanus (lily of the Nile)

Alpinia formosana 'Pinstripe' (ginger lily)

A. Zerumbet 'Variegata'

Alstroemeria psittacia (Peruvian lily)

Arum italicum

Begonia popenoei

Bletilla striata (ground orchid)

B. striata 'Alba'

Chlorophytum comusum 'Magor' (hardy spider plant)

Clivia miniata

C. miniata 'Yellow'

Curcuma inodora (hidden lily)

Dianella tasmanica 'Variegata' (flax lily)

D. caerula

Elettaria cardamomum

Habranthus texanus

H. tubispathus (*Zephyranthes robusta*)

Haemanthus (blood lily)

Hedychium coronarium (butterfly ginger lily)

H. flavum

H. Gardneranum (Kahili ginger)

Hemerocallis (daylily)

Hymenocallis liriosme 'Tropical Giant' (spider lily)

Iris

I. ensata variegata

I. fulva

I. hexagona

I. Pseudacorus

Kaempferia pulchra 'Silver Spot' (resurrection lily)

K. rotunda 'Asian Crocus'

Lilium formosum (candlestick lily)

Narcissus

N. Campernellii

Nymphaea (water lilies)

Polygonatum odoratum Thunbergii 'Variegata' (Solomon's seal)

Reineckia carnea

Rohdea japonica 'Yahazu Yan Jaku' (lily of China, sacred lily)

Rhodophiala bifida (oxblood lily)

R. sifida

Zantedeschia aethiopica (calla lily)

Zephyranthes candida

Z. grandiflora

FERNS

Adiantum capillus-veneris (Southern maidenhair)

Athyrium nipponicum 'Pictum' (Japanese painted)

Arachniodes simplicior 'Variegata' (Indian holly)

Cyrtomium Fortunei

Dicksonia antarctica (Tasmanian tree fern)

Dryopteris erythrosora (Japanese shield)

D. ludoviciana (Southern or Florida shield or wood)

Platycerium Ellisii (staghorn fern)

Polystichum polyblepharum (Korean tassel)

Pteris multifida (Huguenot fern)

Rumohra adiantiformis (leather fern)

Selaginella uncinata

Thelypteris kunthii (widespread maiden)

GRASSES AND BAMBOO

Carex orithopoda 'Variegata' (sedge)

Liriope 'Giant Blue'

L. 'Pee Dee Ingot'

Muhlenbergia dumosa

Ophiopogon (mondo grass)

O. Jaburan 'Gyoku Ryu'

O. planiscapus 'Arabicus'

O. 'Tears of Gold'

HERBACEOUS PERENNIALS AND ANNUALS

Aspidistra elatior

A. elatior 'Variegata'

Aquilegia canadensis (columbine)

A. chrysantha

Capsicum (pepper)

Clerodendrum ugandense

Coleus 'Black Magic'

C. 'Inky Fingers'

C. 'Penny'

C. 'Swirling Skirts'

Cuphea microspetala

Dracaene

Echeveria (hen-and-chickens)

Eupatorium coelestinum (hardy ageratum)

Helleborus foetidus

H. orientalis

Impatiens

Justicia Brandegeana (shrimp plant)

Kalimeris pinnatidifa (Boltonia)

Lespedeza Thunbergii 'Albaflora'

Ligularia tussilaginea 'Argentea'

L.tussilaginea 'Aureo-maculata'

Ludwigia sedoides

Lysimachia Nummularia 'Aurea'

Nepeta (catmint)

Odontonema strictum

Oenothera (evening primrose)

Pentas lanceolata

Phlox divaricata louisiana 'Alba'

P. divaricata 'Frances Parker'

P. paniculata

Plectranthus argentatus

Polygonatum odoratum Thunbergii 'Variegatum' (Solomon's-seal)

Plumbago auriculata

Rehmannia angulata

Rosmarinus officinalis (rosemary)

Rudbeckia laciniata 'Herbstrome'

R. maxima

Ruellia Brittoniana 'Chi Chi' (Mexican petunia, breakfast plant)

Salvia guaranitica

S. x 'Indigo Spires'

S. involucrata

S. leucantha (Mexican bush sage)

S. madrensis

S. miniata

S. uliginosa

S. vanhoutii

Saxifraga stolonifera (strawberry begonia)

Sedum

Tagetes lemmonii

T. lucida (Mexican marigold)

Talinum paniculatum 'Kingswood Gold'

Torenia

Tovara virginiana 'Painter's Palette'

Tulbaghia violacea (society garlic)

T. violacea variegata

Viola hederacea

Zephyranthes candida (rain lily)

Z. grandiflora

ROSES

'Abraham Darby' (David Austin)

'Blush' (noisette)

'Cecile Brunner' (polyantha)

'Cornelia' (musk)

'Duchesse de Brabant' (tea)

'Mme. Alfred Carriere' (noisette)

'Mme. Joseph Schwartz' (tea)

'Mrs. Dudley Cross' (tea)

'Perle d'Or' (polyantha)

'Reve d'Or' (noisette)

'Rosette Delizy' (tea)

'Sombreuilo' (tea)

'Trier' (rambler, hybrid musk)

SHRUBS AND TREES

Acer

A. palmatum 'Bloodgood'

Agarista

Aucuba japonica

Azalea

Buxus Harlandii (boxwood)

B. microphylla 'Becketts'

B.microphylla 'Kingsville Dwarf'

B.microphylla 'Wintergreen'

B.sempervirens

Calycanthus floridus (Carolina Allspice)

Camellia japonica 'Elegans Champagne'

C. Sasanqua

Chionanthus virginicus (fringe tree)

Citrus 'Meyeri Lemon'

Cornus florida (dogwood)

Danae racemosa (Alexandrian laurel)

Daphne odora

Euphorbia cotinifolia

Eriobotrya japonica (Loquat, Japanese plum)

Fatsia japonica

Gardenia jasminoides

Hydrangea arborescens 'Annabelle'

H. 'Frances Parker's Best White'

H. macrophylla 'Blue Billow'

H. macrophylla 'Blue Wave'

H. macrophylla 'Mariesii'

H. macrophylla 'Niger'

H. quercifolia 'Snowflake'

H. serrata 'Greyswood'

Ilex (holly)

I. x attenuata 'East Palatka'

I. x attenuata 'Savannah'

I. cornuta 'Burfordii Nana'

Illicium anisatum

I. henryi

I.Mexicanum

I. parviflorum

Laurus nobilis (bay)

Leucothoe populifolia

Ligustrum lucidum

Magnolia grandiflora

M. grandiflora 'Little Gem'

M. Soulangiana

M. stellata

M. virginiana (sweetbay)

Mahonia 'Arthur Menzies'

M. Bealei

M. x 'Charity'

M. japonica

M. lomariifolia (Burmese)

M. x media 'Lionel Fortescue'

Nandina domestica

Osmanthus americanus

O. aurantiacus

O. fragrans (tea olive)

O. x Fortunei 'San Jose'

O. heterophyllus 'Gulftide'

O. heterophyllus 'Variegatus'

Parkinsonia aculeata (Jerusalem thorn)

Photinia serrulata

Podocarpus macrophyllus 'Maki'

Punica Granatum 'Nana' (dwarf pomegranate)

Quercus virginiana (Southern live oak)

Rhododendron (azalea, rhododendron)

R. austrinum (Florida flame azalea)

R. canescens (Florida pinxter azalea)

Sarcococca Hookerana (sweet box)

S. ruscifolia

Serissa foetida

Teucrium fruticans (tree germander)

Tibouchina granulosa (glory bush)

T. Urvilleana

TROPICALS AND SUBTROPICALS

Abutilon pictum (flowering maple)

Acanthus mollis

Alocasia macrorrhiza (giant elephant's ear)

Brugmansia suaveolens 'Orange'

Calathea burle-marxii

Canna 'Bengal Tiger'

C. 'Freckles'

Cassia alata

Cestrum elegans

C. nocturnum (night-blooming jessamine)

C. Parqui (willow-leaved jessamine)

Citrus calamondin (x citrofortunella mitis)

Clerodendrum speciosissimum

C. ugandense

Colocasia antiquorum 'Illustris' (black leaf taro)

C. esculenta 'Fontanesia'

C. esculenta 'Black Magic'
Costus amazonicus 'Variegata' (spiral ginger)
Elettaria Cardamomum
Ensete ventricosum 'Red Stripe' (Abyssinian banana)
Galphimia glauca
Jatropha integerrima
Musa (banana)
Ricinus communis (castor bean)
Tibouchina granulosa

VINES

Ampelopsis brevipedunculata 'Elegans' (porcelain berry)
Clematis Armandii
Ficus nipponicum
Hedera (ivy)
Podranea Ricasoliana (pink trumpet vine)
Solanum jasminoides
Solanum Seaforthianum (blue potato vine)

Trachelospermum asiaticum
T. jasminoides
T. jasminoides 'Madison'

T. jasminoides 'Variegata'
Wisteria sinensis

The Garden of the William Korber House

For almost fifteen years, Dr. and Mrs. Robert Cathcart spoke of their gardening efforts as "frustrating at best." When they moved to the house in 1975, the yard in back was in use as a neighborhood basketball court, and it remained a playground until their own young children were grown. The area had been designed with low maintenance in mind: narrow borders containing camellias and azaleas surrounded a slab of six-inch thick concrete imbedded with slate. The only landscape feature of any interest was a sixty-foot southern magnolia that dominated the far end of the lot.

When Hurricane Hugo toppled this enormous old tree, serious ideas of installing an entirely new garden were entertained. Seven months before the storm, Mrs. Cathcart had enrolled in a short course given by landscape architects Hugh and Mary Palmer Dargan and sponsored by her garden club. Entitled "Instruction by Lecture and Studio in the Fine Art of Residential Landscape Design," it was an eye-opener and a fascinating exercise. Each participant measured and took notes on her own garden and had scale drawings executed by a local blueprint firm. Each gardener's needs, goals, and ideas were given attention, along with advice on walls, paving, structure, plant material, and recommended reading.

Mrs. Cathcart had been making sketches and taking notes from gardening books and magazines for several years, but was singularly inspired by the well-known garden of her friend and neighbor, Mrs. Ben Scott Whaley. "I kept visiting and taking notes," she recalls, "and finally realized that one of the most appealing elements of its design was the repeated use of circles and curves." After putting their ideas on paper, the couple had a much better idea of what they wanted for their garden.

The storm became the catalyst for engaging the Dargans, who were also asked to incorporate major home renovations into the final plan. French doors opening onto a terrace and an entrance from the kitchen were included in the drawings. A small goldfish pond and fountain became a focal point to be seen and heard from the new family room addition. Garden storage, however, presented a challenge.

Hugh Dargan devised a clever solution: he designed and built a large arched and trellised arbor containing hidden storage for rakes, fertilizer, and other necessities, then planted the stunning and hardy butterfly rose (*Rosa chinensis* 'Mutabilis') to climb and soften the structure. Along the driveway, places for garbage cans, a lawnmower, and other tools were provided by triple chest-high paneled cupboards. These are twelve feet long, three-and-a-half feet wide, have a hinged tin roof for ac-

FACING PAGE: *The garden in early spring.*

44

cess, and are painted to match the house. The paved driveway along the porch side of the house allows parking and is attractive enough, with its handsome painted wooden gates and neat landscaping, for an additional entertaining area.

The immediate impact of the overall garden is color. A flowerbed overflowing with bright seasonal annuals, perennials, and bulbs dominates the street entrance. The shape of this bed, roughly that of a fish, is necessary in order to allow maximum sunlight and access; it is amusing that the men in the family happen to be avid anglers. Generously wide borders curving around a petite oval lawn are packed with more color.

Mrs. Cathcart enjoys taking advantage of every possible gardening space. Even in the shadiest areas, carefully chosen plants thrive, and are a combination of the unusual and the traditional. Small maples and a trio of dogwoods lend seasonal hues, and a replacement for the magnolia lost in the storm is growing well. A variety of potted plants allows for moveable color, especially when spring-blooming azaleas return to their uniform modest green. Pots also provide extra space for herbs and salad greens. More containers of annuals and perennials spill over on the porch and windowsills. "We had just *longed* for a garden," says Mrs. Cathcart, "and ours does not require too much maintenance, especially with the help of an automatic watering system. I'm so pleased with the design. The sunny 'blooming' bed, as I call it, is my very favorite feature."

The Garden of the George Lusher House

In a city boasting a cornucopia of eighteenth- and nineteenth-century dwellings, the George Lusher House stands out as a special beauty. Built around 1810, it is a brick single house with a slate roof, dormers, pretty porches, and exquisite arched fanlights. Set far back from the street on a generous lot behind a tall white picket fence and flanked by palmettos, it has an exotic West Indian flavor.

A patterned garden in an oval shape formalizes the front entrance and is kept simple, which allows the handsome house to be the focal point. A crushed oyster shell path surrounds a solid oval bed of dwarf nandina shrubs. To the south, a graveled driveway extends along the length of the house, its kitchen building, and garage. Beyond these structures lies a St. Augustine grass lawn surrounded by typical Lowcountry plantings of azaleas and camellias, overlooked by a flagstone terrace with comfortable seating. In early spring, a particularly fine mature fringe tree specimen *(Chionanthus virginicus)* is a soft cloud of white floating against the northern horizon.

Two sunny plots, bordered by the driveway and brick walkways in front of the kitchen, serve as a vegetable garden which is the envy of the neighborhood. No fence is necessary to protect it from deer or rabbits, and it is planted in a pretty pattern with whimsical plant markers.

The red banana trees flanking the front and side entrances add to the slightly tropical feel of the property. Pink mandevilla vine looks lovely against the white fence, and a stunning collection of ginger lilies, including hedychiums and *Alpinia Zerumbet* (the pink porcelain lily), has been in the garden for many years. Two generations ago, the owner's sister lived across the street in the Hannah Heyward House and enjoyed sharing many of the plants now thriving in both gardens, notably the gingers growing thickly along the high brick walls. Other, more tender tropicals such as hibiscus and daturas are successfully grown in large pots while hardy perennials line the southern exposure along the drive. They seem to appreciate the additional sunlight resulting from the removal of a huge live oak which used to be at the entrance to the lawn and terrace before it succumbed to damage sustained during Hurricane Hugo. Pear trees line part of the northern exposure of the drive and are under-planted with shade-tolerant nandinas, hydrangeas, and other resilient shrubs. The pears produce heavily for the relishes, chutneys, and preserves the owner enjoys making.

The most unusual feature of the garden is the clever use of smilax vine, whose

FACING PAGE: *The George Lusher house, circa 1810.*

48

shiny greens are traditionally used for mantle and other decorations at Christmastime. This thorny, semi-tropical rambler can be a serious nuisance if left to climb all over shrubs and trees. The owner's mother had allowed the vine to grow along the porch but when her son and daughter-in-law moved in and were painting, the vine was peeled away from the banisters, cut back and balled-up to get it out of the way. It occurred to the present owner's wife—the gardener in the family—to carefully train one substantial piece up each porch column, then to the center of the porch bays, where it is woven into large balls and allowed to dangle, forming her fascinating signature "hanging baskets" that enhance the island influence found in this wonderful old garden.

ABOVE: *Entrance to the back garden, accented by the golden-spotted leaves of aucuba.* LEFT: *Hanging "baskets" formed of smilax and pots filled with red hibiscus and geraniums decorate the porch.*

A Garden on Meeting Street

In 1990, Dr. and Mrs. Layton McCurdy moved into a Neo-Georgian style "single" house built in the early 1900s. Set far enough back from the sidewalk to have a small front garden, it also has the east-west layout typical of many of the residences in this historic district: a driveway abutting the northern facade of the house next door, leading into a long and narrow-walled garden behind the house. The current garden grew out of Mrs. McCurdy's involvement with Charleston's gardening community.

Mrs. McCurdy, who has always enjoyed gardening and community projects, went on the board of The Florence Crittenton Program of South Carolina in 1992 to help with fund raising. Florence Crittenton aims "to provide comprehensive health, education, and social services to single parents and their infants." The board members wanted the fund raising to tie in with their purpose and thought a gardening theme might work well. While living for a time in Philadelphia, Mrs. McCurdy had experience in an organization that did marketing for the Philadelphia Flower Show, and she suggested a comprehensive garden event with an emphasis on both education and bringing the community together.

Now going into its tenth year, the Charleston Garden Festival has moved from its beginnings at a cruiseship passenger terminal to the Gaillard Municipal Auditorium, where it draws thousands of visitors over several days each fall. There are elaborate exhibition gardens inside and out and dozens of local and out-of-town vendor booths selling everything from plants to tools to furniture. A symposium featuring nationally known garden experts is the main educational focus, but there are also city and plantation garden tours, daily lectures, demonstrations, and a gala party. A rare plant auction is a popular event, and an evergreen maze that was a delight to both children and adults was a feature in 1998.

"I chaired the Festival for two years," says Mrs. McCurdy, "and became particularly interested in growing perennials, which was the latest buzzword in the city after Hurricane Hugo. In Philadelphia we lived in a high-rise and had lots of herbs and topiaried plants in pots on patios. Our garden in Charleston was largely lawn and annuals. Then we were asked to put our garden on tour, and I realized that lots of people expected me to be a good gardener and that *really* piqued my interest," she laughs.

"My first step in refurbishing the landscape was to get some good advice and to remove a dying crab apple, a large oak that was blocking the sun, and a loquat that

FACING PAGE: *Deep purple verbena contrasts with yellow wallflowers.*

was so messy it was a hindrance. I asked Jim Martin, the Director of Horticultural Operations for the State Botanical Garden, whom I had met through the Festival, to help with the plant material. I like unusual plants—surprises—in the garden and I love to experiment with new material." There is a greenhouse at the back of the lot where she can coddle the orchids which she admits now take a backseat to the perennials. "I didn't change the hardscape of the garden except to add a pergola," she continues. "I don't feel that I have a very strong sense of design and I wanted the plants themselves to make my gardening statement for me."

The design, however, is lovely. The rectangular front flowerbed has recently been redesigned and planted by Jim Martin, using *heteropterys glabra*, giant liriope (*Liriope muscari* 'Evergreen Giant'), sago palms *(Cycas revoluta)*, spider lilies *(Zephyranthes radiata)*, espaliered sansanqua 'Cleopatra' against the house, and the

FACING PAGE: *A decorative birdbath.* ABOVE: *The long and narrow garden is typical of this area in the Historic District.*

low spreading shrub *Euonymus Fortunei* 'Colorata' (purple leaf wintercreeper). As one goes back to the garden through the brick-paved drive and the L-shaped area opening out behind the house, one sees a series of pots of all sizes filled with a huge variety of plants and fruit-bearing citrus trees. Some of the pots contain sweet potato vines, ornamental grasses, variegated agave, yellow wallflower *(Erysimum Perofskianum),* witch hazel *(Hamamelis x intermedia* 'Arnold Promise'), and juniper *(Juniperus squamata).* Three standard laurels kept to a height of about five feet anchor a newly planted bed in front of the carriage house, which has a southern exposure. Beneath the laurels is a rhythmic pattern of soft yellow lantana, deep baby-blue plumbago *(Plumbago auriculata* 'Imperial Blue'), and river oats *(Chasmanthium latifolium). Cestrum aurantiacum* and *Clitoria Ternatea* 'Blue Sails' give orange and purple accents. *Clerodendrum myricoides* 'Ugandense' is one of the newer perennial varieties introduced by Mr. Martin. A low wall with a gate separates this long stretch behind the house into two separate gardens and underscores the progression from formal to informal.

The back garden is a rectangle surrounded by walls and buildings. More or less divided by a curving path thickly edged with mondo grass *(Ophiopogon)* into a shade garden on the south and more exuberant deep sunny beds on the north, it features a small goldfish pond in the center with a pergola-covered sitting area off to the sunny side. In May, the lavender and white spikes of foxgloves complement tall yellow iris and spires of vivid blue delphiniums. Fat-flowered yellow daylilies, true forget-me-nots *(Myosotis scorpioides* 'Semperflorens'), and roses continue the yellow, blue, and white scheme. For contrast, there are touches of burgundy loropetalum, purple-leaf crinum lilies and spiderwort *(Tradescantia), Ajuga* 'Burgundy Glow', coleus, and a wide range of hellebores. By fall, many of the more unusual perennials will be in bloom. There are white Philippine lilies, sacred lilies *(Rohdea japonica), Stachyurus, Plectranthus amboinicus, Rudbeckia nitida* 'Herbstsonne,' *Cordyline, Alternanthera, Angelonia, Hamelia patens* (firebush), and newer cultivars of aster, verbena, gingers, and anise.

Mrs. McCurdy recently increased the number of her flowerbeds by taking out a low holly hedge opposite the carriage house, and has made a pretty fern garden underneath the tree on the strip of grass between the sidewalk and the house. She likes to layer color and texture by using bulbs overplanted with annuals to save space. Borrowed views can also help. "I love having gardeners as neighbors," she remarks. "I don't have the space for so many lovely things and particularly appreciate the banana and eucalyptus trees just over our property line. I still want to put the brilliant yellow of a cassia at the very back of the garden and have several challenging areas which will keep me busy," she adds. When it comes to new plants, she is always enthusiastic about trying to make room for more.

The Garden of the Elizabeth Petrie House

By the early 1700s, there were a number of established pleasure gardens on the peninsula. One of these, once used for concerts and planted with many orange trees, was divided into building lots in 1767 by Alexander Petrie, a silversmith. His widow, Elizabeth, lived in a small wooden "single" house built on one of the lots by his estate. In this architectural style peculiarly seen in Charleston, a one-room wide house sits perpendicular to the street and often has a porch (or "piazza") facing west or south. The porch is entered from the street and the house is entered through a central door from the porch.

The Petrie House is separated from the building next door by a space just wide enough for a driveway that runs west along the building to the garden behind the house. There is no eighteenth-century documentation describing a garden here, but early plans from similar lots show a practical yard divided into rectangular plots for flowers, vegetables, and herbs. Utilitarian outbuildings, called dependencies, were common, and the present owners, Dr. and Mrs. H. Biemann Othersen, received a box of pottery, china, and glass fragments excavated from the area where the privies had been located on the property.

What remains of the current brick outline of the garden design is attributed to the landscape architect Loutrel Briggs, who also worked on several other gardens in the immediate neighborhood. As the visitor enters from the drive through a wrought iron gate, there is a neat lawn symmetrically surrounded by a low rectangular brick border with graceful French curves, all edged in boxwood. When the Othersens bought the house twenty years ago, the garden was deeply shaded by hollies, magnolias, and a huge live oak in the northwest corner with branches that also shaded at least four other gardens. Traditional plantings of azaleas, camellias, and tea olives were maturing into trees, rather than shrubs.

Hurricane Hugo let in light. A thirty-to-forty foot holly tree simply disappeared from the garden during the storm. The Othersens thought they recognized it on the street about a block away, but there was so much debris, it was difficult to identify. The oak survived, but had been severely damaged, and the neighbors' magnolia that had kept out much of the southern sunlight had been destroyed. Fortunately, the garden took the brunt of the storm; the northern windows of the house had been sucked out of their frames, but the house had little damage otherwise.

Mrs. Othersen started to clean up the garden immediately. "I had to rely on others

FACING PAGE, TOP: Plantings along the driveway include tulips, which are treated as annuals in our climate.
FACING PAGE, BOTTOM: The live oak over the fountain and back wall survived Hurricane Hugo.

to repair the damage to the house," she remembers, " but I could get on with the garden myself." She had always enjoyed plants that bloomed and favored the vivid colors of sun-loving annuals and perennials, so she began to study catalogs and visit nurseries in search of new ideas for her now open, sunny landscape.

Mary Zahl, a garden designer who had recently moved to Charleston, drew up a plan and suggested eliminating some of the plants which had survived the twelve-inch surge of salt water during the storm, but were not healthy. The best azaleas and camellias were dug up and moved to the back of the garden where there was still shade. Mary also drew the designs for a simple arbor and for the four ironwork arches installed along the drive. Pyracantha had grown against the building facade, but had failed from Hugo damage. Mrs. Othersen created the zig-zag brick border beneath the arches and decided to install a raised fish pond as a focal point in the center of the back wall of the property. Both Mary Zahl and Peggy Smalls helped with choosing and arranging plants, especially some of the perennials. Those two designers have left Charleston and now Beverly Rivers is using her talents to help keep the garden lush and blooming while not allowing the trees and shrubs to get out-of-hand.

Holly Ferns spill into the fountain.

There was an unusual tree, a *Ziziphus Jujuba* (jujube), planted as a lawn specimen,

which had survived the hurricane. It was in poor health, but had a twisted trunk around which Mrs. Othersen planted a thorny 'Mermaid' rose (a hybrid bracteata). A high wind eventually toppled the jujube tree, but the 'Mermaid' rose thrived. A pyramidal wooden trellis was built to support the rose, which is currently under consideration for permanent removal because its blossoms are best viewed only from the second or third storey of the house and it is so thorny that it is "frankly dangerous" to prune, says Mrs. Othersen.

More sun exposure has allowed the owners to grow the variety of Mandarin oranges that were first planted here in the 1700s. A recent harvest boasted over one hundred Satsumas. Herbs are thriving, especially a rosemary shrub by the back door that is twelve feet wide and five feet tall. Mrs. Othersen enjoys discovering new plant material and trying different combinations of annuals and perennials. Hollyhocks grow for her, as do salvias, lantana, gingers, daisies, and old roses. "I am a spontaneous gardener," explains Mrs. Othersen. "I tend to work in spurts and when I see a space that needs a plant, I head for the nursery. My husband enjoys gardening in a supervisory way, but I hope to entice him to be more 'hands-on' when he retires."

Four ironwork arches support roses and create interest along a wall.

61

The Garden of the James L. Petigru Law Office

"Bone-empty" is how Mrs. Irénée DuPont May describes the courtyard as she first saw it twenty-two years ago. "There was a pomegranate tree and there was a camellia 'Pink Perfection,' both of which are still alive, but the rest of the garden was a jungle of weeds." The "courtyard" constitutes the space between two buildings which make up the old Petigru Law Office property designed by the architect Edward Brickell White and completed by 1849. Petigru's own pleasure garden was originally on a lot directly across the street.

During the restoration of the property, which included removing an unsightly and unnecessary wooden appendage to the main building, a stone terrace was added and a small pool was created as a focal point. "The courtyard just evolved over the years," says Mrs. May, who was an interior designer from Wilmington, Delaware. "I was not used to southern plants and was surprised at how quickly everything grew. I bought the huge 'Natchez' crape myrtle in the corner of the property at a plant auction up north, because my mother was from Natchez. I thought it was a dwarf variety," she confesses.

Interestingly, the charming little space contains a surprising number of plants with large foliage or large growth habits, such as crinum lilies, *Colocasia* (elephant's-ear), *Tetrapanax papyriferus* (rice paper plant), a *Magnolia grandiflora*, and a palm tree. Also among the plants are acanthus, lilies of the Nile *(Agapanthus)*, fatsia, mahonias, hostas, camellias, and sasanquas. Fragrant flowers are particular favorites and include *Daphne odora*, *Osmanthus fragrans* (tea olive), gardenias, loquat, and several varieties of ginger. Corsican mint *(Mentha Requienii)* does well as a groundcover and ferns thrive in the shade, as do hydrangeas, viburnum, and hellebores. "I'm of the 'just one more' school of gardening," she admits.

In 1998, Mrs. May decided to refurbish. Her chief concern was that the grass was dying in spots where it got too much shade. Sheila Wertimer, a local landscape architect, was consulted and came up with a plan to extend the paving as well as to plant Algerian ivy in place of some of the grass. Mrs. Wertimer also had her blacksmith make an iron arch for a visual separation between the main courtyard and the smaller one tucked into the "L" of the brick two-storeyed guest house/studio that sits behind the main house. "Sheila provided the 'third eye' that I needed in the garden and helped me upgrade my plant list by having the courage to pull out the ones which just weren't working," says Mrs. May.

FACING PAGE: *View of the courtyard from the studio.*

62

BELOW: *A decorative planter.*
FACING PAGE: *The courtyard
and its quartet of cedars.*

The dominant feature and glory of the courtyard is the stunning quartet of forty-foot cedars around the fountain in the pool. The fountain was added about six years ago, but the cedars were planted by Mrs. May when she first started working on the garden. In 1989, Hurricane Hugo's winds twisted the cedars right out of the ground. All four were lying in the courtyard, battered and broken, when Mrs. May returned to the city a week later to assess the damage to her property. Sadly, she instructed her gardener, Earl, to haul them out to the street with the rest of the storm debris, and she left town again.

Two weeks later, Earl called her with the news that the cedars were back in place. He had pruned them and enlisted the help of a crew of family and friends to re-dig the holes and wrestle the trees upright again into their old spots. Touched by his dedication and tremendous effort, Mrs. May gently assured Earl that she deeply appreciated his labor even though she had her doubts that the cedars could survive, much less ever look the same. "Ma'am," Earl stated confidently, "da sun gwine ta draw 'em." And it did. Healthy and shapely once again, the cedars echo the magnificent spire of St. Michael's Episcopal Church a few hundred feet away.

A Pleasure Garden

Mary Martha Blalock's enthusiasm for gardening is contagious. Not only does she grow and arrange flowers, but she also gives horticultural tours, helps maintain the Charleston Museum's Heyward-Washington House garden, volunteers for several local garden-related organizations, helps bring interesting garden speakers to the city and entertains them, and travels throughout the South to attend garden symposiums and visit plant nurseries and gardens. Years ago, she became part of a small group of students who took courses such as "woody ornamentals," "annuals," and "the new American garden" at a local college and who still meet about once a month for discussion and exchange. In 1983, she wrote the botanical notes for the City of Charleston's official tour guide manual.

Mrs. Blalock's present garden is located all around her late Victorian townhouse, which is situated on a busy street. The area burned in the fire of 1861 and was rebuilt during the 1870s and 1880s as a residential area of modified single houses with bay windows and little Victorian front yards.

In 1989, Hurricane Hugo destroyed the entire front garden and left only a few tough trees and shrubs in the driveway to the west and in the small lot behind the house to the south. A good portion of the roof was also found in the back yard. Not too long after the storm, Frances Parker, an expert gardener from Beaufort, South Carolina, came to visit the Blalocks and stood with them looking out a window at the wreck below. She suggested a tunnel of fruit trees with two ten-foot square beds on either side and a deep shade bed at the far end of the garden. A narrow lawn and flagstone paths would tie it all together. Mary Zahl, a garden designer who had recently moved to Charleston and who had inspired Mrs. Blalock with a presentation on the use of color, was asked to draw up the plans.

The plan worked well, for, as Mrs. Blalock explains, "This is a flower arranger's garden, but it is also a collector's garden." Every day, at least one bucketful of blossoms and greens is picked for arrangements; this has the added benefit of keeping the pruning under control. One of the main beds displays blue, red, and yellow flowering plants, while the other is filled with pastel colors. Both beds contain some old-fashioned roses and both feature the fountain-like white 'Frau Karl Druschki,' which blooms several times a year. Red is a favorite color, and is particularly effective against the deep slate blue of the surrounding privacy fence. Most of the plant varieties are chosen for their value as cut flowers and include herbs such as the feathery

FACING PAGE: *Old roses and honeysuckle intertwine on an arbor. In the background, the yellow trumpets of bignonia, or cat's claw vine, drape across the garage.*

One of Mrs. Blalock's front-door arrangements in a signature Charleston sweetgrass basket. FACING PAGE, TOP: *The knot garden.* FACING PAGE, BOTTOM: *Pots provide extra planting space in the driveway.*

copper fennel and lacy rue. Riveroats, grasses such as the red pennisetum, and plants which produce attractive seed heads are grown, too. There are about a dozen different salvias, which come in hot as well as pastel colors and are heat tolerant.

Some of the more unusual plants have been collected from abandoned homesites, received as gifts, or acquired on trips. The director of Mount Vernon gave Mrs. Blalock celosia seeds from George Washington's garden, a visitor sent wisteria native to South Carolina, and a *Camellia sinensis* (tea plant) came from Hemingway, South

Carolina, via Michaux's 1787 garden near Charleston. A friend shared a native aster, and several other native plants were found in the garden and saved, or were found at specialty nurseries. "Passalong" cuttings and rootings from friends' gardens flourish. Mrs. Blalock has flowers from Elizabeth Lawrence's garden and larkspur from Mount Vernon. There are also unusual annuals and shrubs, such as *Duranta repens,* with its lavender flowers and dramatic drupes of yellow berries, the pink *Cestrum elegans,* and white *Patrinia.*

Collecting many varieties of the same species is an ongoing hobby. There are over a dozen different salvias in all colors, numerous hydrangeas, and altheas. Old roses include 'Champney's Pink Cluster' (the first noisette), 'Old Blush,' 'Lamarque,' 'Souvenir De La Malmaison,' 'Marie Pavié,' 'Jose's White' (a found rose from Puerto Rico), 'Trinity' (the Bermuda 'mystery' rose), 'Trier' (a hybrid musk), and *Rosa palustris scandens* (the swamp rose). Fruit trees include: tangerine, kumquat, fig, pineapple pear, loquat (Japanese plum), and the hardy orange *(Poncirus trifoliata).* Kitchen herbs spill from pots on the back steps and are mixed in with other plants.

In the shade are shrubs, vines, and plants selected particularly for white blossoms, as well as tropical purple elephant's ears, mahogany fern, hostas, acanthus, and hydrangeas. Euphorbia, helleborus, *Iris foetidissima*, pulmonaria, teucrium, and tiarella are growing in dry shade. White Beauty *(Callicarpa leucocarpa)* is a recent acquisition.

Mrs. Blalock helped to install the knot garden at the Heyward-Washington House. The eighteenth-century-style formal garden behind the house is maintained by The Garden Club of Charleston, and displays plants that would have been in the garden in 1790, when George Washington was a guest there. When it was time to replant the small space in front of her house, she also used *Serissa foetida* for the outline of her own knot garden: an oval flanked by semicircles, punctuated by a pair of topiary bay laurels. Low yaupon holly *(Ilex vomitoria)* pyramids add another touch of formality. The display of plants changes seasonally. In the fall, perennials including salvias, plumbago, *Ruellia* (breakfast plant) and heather are cut back and overplanted with annuals such as sweet alyssum, pansies, and larkspur. Close by, an old chaste tree *(Vitex Agnus-castus)* supports a chocolate vine *(Akebia quinata).* When a delivery truck hit the tree in the sidewalk in front of the house, the City, much to Mrs. Blalock's delight, replaced it with a palm from the buffalo cage at Hampton Park, where the zoo was being demolished.

Now this inveterate gardener is planning to design a perennial cutting garden on the grounds of the Charleston Museum's Joseph Manigault House, built in 1803. The Garden Club of Charleston has largely restored the garden to its 1820 appearance and the hope is to provide year-round material for flower arrangements appropriate for the period of the house. It will surely be a glorious display.

The Garden of the Poyas-Edwards House

I t was inevitable that Mrs. Edward H. Sparkman would become a gardener. During her childhood in south Georgia, she was inspired and instructed by her grandmother, "Miss Ida," a well-known and frequently consulted local gardener. "Miss Ida" required the young members of her family to read articles about gardening and help with the planting. She also took the children on frequent visits to Callaway Gardens, then owned by a close friend, in the years before the twelve thousand acre estate opened to the public in 1952. Later, at the age of twenty-seven, Mrs. Sparkman became the youngest member of an established garden club in Florida. She particularly enjoyed flower arranging and was intrigued by the huge variety of available plant material. Arranging soon became a favorite pastime, and subsequently influenced her choices of flowers and shrubs in her own gardens.

The family moved into the Poyas-Edwards house in Charleston in 1984. The residence, a Greek Revival structure built about 1834 on a lot measuring one hundred forty by forty feet, is patterned on the Charleston single house plan: one room wide

BELOW: Deep red azaleas stand out against the "Charleston Green" paint on the carriage house trim. Hurricane Hugo's floodwaters came up to the base of the wall plaque to the left of the door.

FACING PAGE: *Early spring view into the garden.*

with a central hall, several storeys high, and entered from the street through a side porch.

Renovations began in 1987 and included landscaping. "The bones of the garden were actually very good," Mrs. Sparkman recalls. "We just emphasized them." A hedge of the hardy winter blooming *Camellia Sasanqua* was established at a right angle to the entrance, dividing the garden into two sections and providing privacy from the street for a lawn and flagstone terrace beyond. Dark green trellis was added to the top of a wall to help camouflage the imposing pastel facade of a neighboring building at the end of the property. A handsome old family urn became a centerpiece and focal point where the lawn and terrace intersected.

Now, as one enters the garden through a low wall and gate, an asymmetrical paisley-patterned boxwood hedge sets a formal tone, offset by the informality of herbs and pots of annuals and perennials placed in sunny spots. The first of two sitting areas is just beyond, separated from an oval lawn by the high sasanqua hedge. A picturesque brick kitchen building, extending behind the house, faces the lawn and a larger terrace at the very back. In spring, an ornamental cherry dominates the entire garden with a showy burst of pale pink, followed by the deep pink of a crape myrtle in summer. Numerous shade-tolerant shrubs such as gardenia, camellia, nandina, tea olive (*Osmanthus fragrans*), elaeagnus, cleyera, and aucuba fill in under tall hollies.

The two-year-old plantings were making a good start when Hurricane Hugo hit in 1989. Three trees on the west side were brought down and over four feet of salt water covered the property during the storm surge. Months later it was apparent that the garden was not, after all, a total loss. There were many survivors, a large number of native plants among them. Tom Dodd, who had recently started a local nursery specializing in shrubs and trees native to the southeast, was soon consulted.

One of the first installations Dodd suggested was a line of 'Will Fleming' hollies, which resemble Italian cypresses. Adding height and variety, they help define the outline of the garden and soften the bricks of an adjacent three-storeyed house. Little design work was necessary other than creating more paths and adding interesting specimens. Piedmont, Florida, flame and coastal azaleas work well with other native shrubs, including *Agarista populifolia, Cassandra calyculata, Itea virginica, Pinckneya bracteata pubens*, and *Amorpha fruticosa* (false indigo). Among the small trees are *Gardenia lasianthus* (loblolly bay), *Pinckneya bracteata* (fever-tree), and *Franklinia altamaha* (lost Gordonia).

Specimens have been collected on garden club expeditions and other travels. A stop at a farmer's market resulted in the purchase of red and white cultivars of a favorite showy groundcover, *hypoestes*. Along with trips to nurseries and plant exchanges, which are annual events in her garden club, Mrs. Sparkman continues to enjoy studying, arranging, and sharing the many plant species native to this area.

The Garden of the Old St. Michael's Rectory

The wall that used to surround the oldest part of the city of Charleston was torn down in 1717, after the defeat of the Yemassee Indians. Just within the western edge of the fortification, running north-south, was one of the principal streets laid out in 1672. Today, some of Charleston's most beautiful houses and gardens still line the street. Glimpses of the gardens, however, can be difficult, for the imposing residences tend to be contiguous to or only a short distance from the wide sidewalks and the main gardens are behind the houses, usually reached through the house itself or by means of a driveway along the south side of the building.

The old St. Michael's rectory, built by Miller and Fullerton in 1767, is one of several eighteenth-century houses which, remarkably, survive together within a few city blocks. Almost all the lots are long, narrow, and fairly generous for a town space. In this century, the Rectory was completely renovated in the 1940s by the family who occupied it until the present owners acquired it in 1988, a year before Hurricane Hugo.

Because of the hurricane, there were delays in moving into the house on schedule, but it gave the new owners some time to reflect on the work they wanted to do in the garden. "We realized the need for a structure that would provide much-needed storage," notes the owner, "and would anchor the very back of the property" (which abuts a tall brick façade). John Laurens designed for the owners a one-storey brick folly with two arched windows. The structure, which resembles an eighteenth-century orangerie, doubles as a greenhouse in the winter. Mary Zahl was consulted for the design of the hardscape and the placement of major plants. She suggested arranging the property, which is approximately 236 feet deep and roughly 43 feet wide, into three distinct gardens flowing one into the next.

The front garden is about 18 feet wide, and consists of a strip of lawn behind the iron fence along the sidewalk. Roses, plumbago, *salvia leucantha*, and a flowering cherry provide color. At the end of the driveway, which is paved with flagstones and lined on its northern exposure with espaliered pink sasanquas and a delightful assortment of ferns and other shade-tolerant plants, the middle garden opens out into the L formed by the back of the house and its narrower dependency building. A flagstone path continues to the right along the southern side of the kitchen house, where sun-loving annuals and perennials are bedded. To the left is a St. Augustine grass lawn that can tolerate the shade cast by the back side of the Georgian house next

FACING PAGE: *The old St. Michael's rectory, circa 1767.*

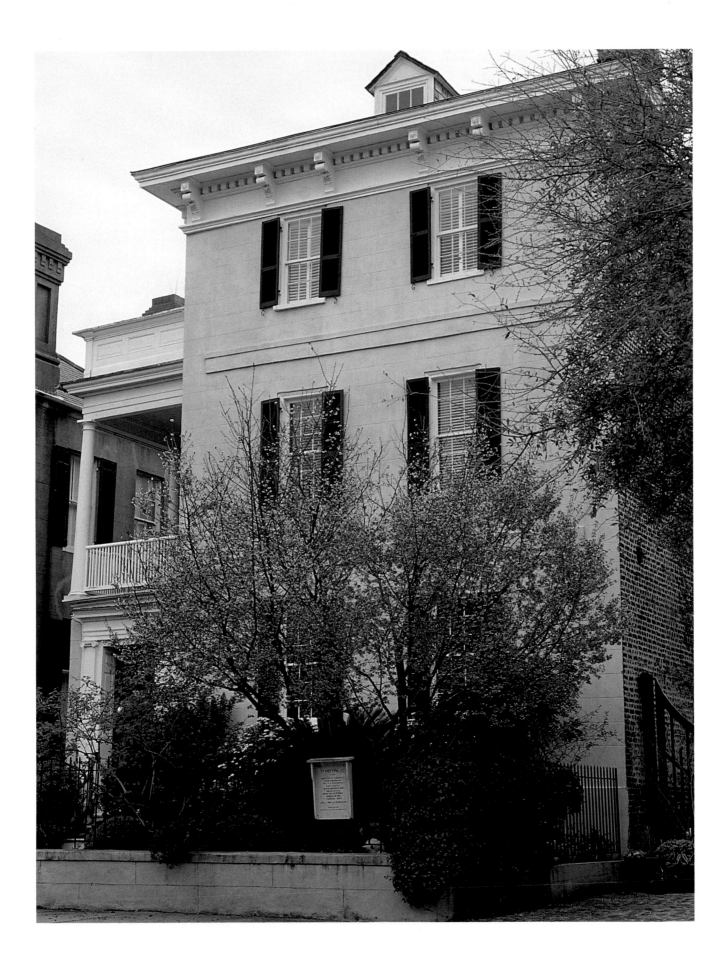

*Bright orange tithonias bloom
in front of the new garden
building.*

door. Lanky 'Will Fleming' hollies at the path edge of the grass help balance the height of the buildings and a few large specimen trees. A pink oleander the owners had wintered inside in Philadelphia is pruned into a five-trunked tree form and leans out over the path. Several old roses, including a Bermuda rose, 'Mrs. Atwood,' are planted and there is a terrace shaded by an old banana shrub *(Michelia Figo)*. White plants are a favorite in this seating area, which is separated from the back garden by a pierced brick wall and a wrought iron gate.

Orange lychnis and tithonia are beautifully displayed against purple-leaved canna and salvia.

Here, in the back, with the orangerie as the focal point, Mary Zahl centered an octagonal goldfish pond and surrounded it with four parterres. On the north-south axis is a pair of wrought iron pergolas, each supporting a gas lantern and red 'Don Juan' roses. But the formality ends with the structures. According to Beverly Rivers, who works with the design of plant material in the garden and helps maintain it, the owner "loves the exuberance and lushness of tropical and semitropical plants within the formal boundaries." He has worked with several garden designers and enjoys the plants each one has introduced.

A variety of tender and tropical plants surrounds the pond. The brilliant yellow bush in the background is Cassia corymbosa.

Even though the garden is at its best in the fall because of the emphasis on perennials and autumn color, there is a carefully planned succession of bloom. Spring favorites include fragrant osmanthus, camellias, a few azaleas, hellebores, bulbs, larkspur, delphinium, foxgloves, stock, and snapdragons, as well as cool season giant mustards and other edibles. A large flowering maple *(Abutilon)* starts off the warmer weather, followed by a riot of cannas, tithonias, orange impatiens, brilliant yellow *Cassia corymbosa,* the exotic purple and red castor bean plant (*Ricinus communis*), various grasses, dramatic peach, white, and purple daturas, colorful coleus, periwinkle blue plumbago, over a dozen varieties of salvias, banana trees, and exorbitant crinum lilies. Orchids have long been a passion and are nurtured in the more controlled environment inside the house.

In the shade, there is a bit more restraint, as the beds contain white wisteria, maidenhair and other ferns, variegated ivies, acanthus, crocosmia, ardisia, lamiastrum, and hydrangeas. Three substantial terra cotta pots arranged in front of the orangerie hold grapefruits that are harvested throughout their season. Lantanas spilling out from the bases of the fruit trees are in keeping with the riot of summer bloom. Lemons and oranges are tucked into a sunny corner near the porch. The owners enjoy unusual plants, many of which came from Frances Parker's nursery in Beaufort, South Carolina, but they especially appreciate those plants which provide berries and cover for the birds and other wildlife found in a city garden.

The Garden of the Anthony Toomer House

In 1796, Anthony Toomer, a Revolutionary War veteran and a master builder, purchased a 40-by-296-foot lot and built on it as an investment. Later additions were made to the building in the nineteenth century, but the lot has remained its original size.

In 1995, Mr. and Mrs. Andrew T. Barrett purchased the property and decided to engage local landscape architect Sheila Wertimer to design a layout for the long, narrow lot. The couple, who had lived in several cities abroad, knew that they wanted to have a parterre garden with an English feel, a swimming pool, a fish pond, and a play area for the children, as well as much-needed garden storage. Five areas evolved, each with its own distinct character: the driveway walk, the kitchen garden, a play area, a formal parterre garden, and the pool garden. The Barretts also asked restoration contractor Richard Marks, rosarian Ruth Knopf, and metal craftsman Rick Averett to assist in the process.

The long garden runs east-west and its main axis is centered on the two-storeyed white-columned porch attached to the south side of the building. Narrower than the house, the dependency buildings also run east-west behind the residence, opening onto the courtyard kitchen garden and the children's play area. A white brick wall separates the property from the neighbor's, whose house is set well back from the street, thereby letting sunshine and air into this area of the garden. In contrast, and a relief in the summer, the driveway is shaded by mature flowering photinia trees reaching over a white picket fence. Pots filled with herbs and flowers line the two courtyard gardens, giving them an informal feel, and there is comfortable outdoor furniture. The kitchen garden also has some sour orange trees and other edibles. Crape myrtles used here are a smaller variety suited to the scale of the wall and outbuildings. Rick Averett fashioned an ironwork cover for a well which was discovered near a hand pump against the wall. The dry well now hosts a variety of ferns (and a collection of the dog's tennis balls). Next to the well is a simple, semicircular goldfish pond with a stream of water splashing into it from a fountain on the wall.

The children's playroom opens out onto the extension of the kitchen garden. It, too, is paved with brick and has a weighted, mobile basketball hoop and a bicycle storage room enclosed by seven-foot high *Podocarpus* (southern yew) hedges. The plants chosen for this area are hardy and prosaic, such as giant liriope.

What follows next, through an opening in a low wall, is a formal pattern garden. A palm-shaded bench sits off to the north side and the path widens for wheelbarrow access to a garden storage shed featuring wooden arched doors. The parterres Mrs. Wertimer designed are four truncated squares surrounding a diamond-shaped bed containing an urn on a pedestal. Slightly unusual in design, the boxwood beds are not hedged in on the sides facing the central diamond, but are open to allow a seasonal choice of plants to spill out onto the walk. Diverting the eye from the back of the house next door, and continuing the formality of this section of the garden, is an iron arch flanked by four horizontal panels of criss-cross wire. Fragrant Confederate jasmine *(Trachelospermun jasminoides)* is trained along the wires. Acanthus plants thrive in the shady corners.

The pool garden is entered through a decorative wrought iron gate beneath an iron arbor entwined in a yellow Lady Banksia rose. Shaded by a *Magnolia soulangiana* and two limbed-up southern yew trees, an inviting stretch of lawn is only a step down from the arbor, with a dark-bottomed pool beyond. The eye-catcher, however, is a stunning, dramatic group of six lofty Italian cypresses planted in a pair of raised beds curving around the end of the pool. Stone steps lead up to a bench in front of a weathered brick wall covered in a cascade of roses.

The cypresses were suggested by Mr. Barrett, who also came up with a practical and highly decorative pattern of grass and stone pavers between the pool and the seating areas. Mrs. Barrett especially enjoys playing with the arrangement of plants within the deep flowerbed running the northern length of the pool garden. Her love of gardening, she says, evolved with the couple's travels. They lived in Dubai, in the United Arab Emirates, where she had to bring in soil to replace the sand and, of course, use irrigation. There she grew bougainvillas, oleanders, periwinkle, portulaca, and all sorts of succulents. In Switzerland they had a small "wrap-around" garden. "The gardens there tended to be very neat, tidy, and extremely colorful, with lots of bulbs, annuals, and seasonal displays," she says. When they moved to London for several years, they only had a small city garden, but she loved it. "We could grow lilacs, fabulous roses, and many varieties of lavender. We could also use plants now familiar to me in Charleston, such as pittosporum and wisteria." The apple trees covered with roses in the orchard at Sissinghurst Castle in England inspired the use of trees as trellises for some of the old roses which Ruth Knopf advised her could tolerate our heat and humidity.

Beverly Rivers also helped Mrs. Barrett choose perennials. The garden already contains plumbago, sedums, daylilies, assorted herbs, artemisia, *Stachys* (lamb's-ears), lantana, iris, monarda, verbena, salvias, and ferns, and Mrs. Barrett is eager to learn more about the wide variety of plants which will grow in our climate and wants to continue trying new placements and combinations throughout the garden, an approach which sounds both fascinating and rewarding.

ABOVE: *A pair of cycads lend a tropical atmosphere in one of the courtyards.* BELOW: *A neighbor's pittosporum is in full, fragrant bloom.Entrance to the kitchen courtyard.* FACING PAGE: *The pool at the Toomer house.*

The Garden of the Doctor
Anthony Vanderhorst Toomer House

Sharon and Richard Densmore purchased the Anthony Vanderhorst Toomer house in Wraggborough just three months before Hurricane Hugo struck in September 1989. Work had already begun on a three-storeyed addition to the early-nineteenth-century building when the storm blew the roof off the main house, damaging all four floors. Instead of the estimated six weeks, it was two years before the family could move in.

The landscape, however, was in no worse shape than before the storm, as little had been done previously. The house sat on a large city lot that extended far back to the north behind the building, but with only a few feet allowance to the east and west. The front yard, though generous, was cut off at an angle by the street and was a challenge to organize in any pattern.

A designer, artist, and collector, Mrs. Densmore was excited about creating her own garden from a "desolate blank slate," as she described the way it looked after the storm. She enlisted the help of landscape architects Hugh and Mary Palmer Dargan for placement of fences, walls, paths, and drainage—or "hardscape"—on the uneven lot, but did all of the design work herself. An extensive library of garden books helped her choose plant material and gave her ideas for what was to become a series of gardens encircling the house.

Starting with the front of the house, Mrs. Densmore drew a plan for an elaborate pattern garden featuring topiary spiral evergreens and a pair of specimen Drake elms set in the centers of symmetrical boxwood-bordered parterres. Wide stone steps and rails covered with white roses lead up to the porch from which the front garden is designed to be viewed. An Italian garden is the theme for the east side of the property, an herb garden lies to the west of the house, and an English cottage garden has the sunny southern exposure at the back of the lot. There is a "ruin" and a shady courtyard with a fountain, and there are several more fountains, a variety of arbors, and even a miniature version of a parterre garden out on the sidewalk. Intimate seating areas are arranged to fill corners or to take advantage of an especially pretty view.

The plants in the garden are an excellent collection of the species and varieties that grow well in the city of Charleston and include native plants as well as recent introductions. The walk along the western side of the house has been planted with a wide variety of herbs, but also with vines familiar to local gardeners. Moon vine, Carolina Jessamine (the South Carolina state flower), Confederate Jasmine, coral

vine, hyacinth bean, and climbing roses reach up through and over a podocarpus privacy hedge and scramble up holly trees.

Entrance to the garden in Wraggsborough.

In shady areas, reliable favorites such as nandina, fatsia, aucuba, mahonia, aspidistra, hydrangea, camellia, and azalea are beautifully arranged and pruned. Mrs. Densmore enjoys pruning the maze of boxwoods and other low hedges herself, and she uses hardy plants that do not require spraying with chemicals. Many diseases and pest problems are solved by careful maintenance and the use of products such as insecticidal soap.

The bold use of color is a trademark of the garden. Not only are there the magenta blossoms of four-o-clocks and the purple trumpets of the breakfast plant (*Ruellia*), but there are cast iron benches and chairs painted the same watermelon pink as the blooms of the crape myrtle trees above. A bright yellow chair lights up a dark area; silver germander and lavender roses share a flowerbed. In addition to a color wheel of blossoms, fruits and berries add more color and texture through the seasons. Pomegranate trees have showy, bright orange blossoms; kumquats fruit in the win-

BELOW: *The birdbath fountain.* FACING PAGE: *A parterre in the herb garden.*

ter; standard-form pyracanthas drip with red-orange berries for months at a time; and the Japanese plum, or loquat, is a reliable producer of edible orange-fleshed fruits. The Drake elms were chosen for their soft chartreuse-colored leaves in early spring, interesting seed pods, and multicolored exfoliating bark.

Lance L. Leader, an expert brick mason, has helped Mrs. Densmore create the effect of a rocky ruin and has installed fountains and a variety of stone and brick-work. He hollowed out an old piece of brownstone for the birdbath fountain at the front gate and recently completed a recessed wall fountain with a shell motif. During the excavation of a concrete driveway, Belgian block was discovered on the property and has been used for some of the paving and for three planters of graduated height along the east side of the house.

A touch of whimsy is around every corner. Birdhouses, birdcages, tables, benches, and chairs are scattered throughout the garden, but so are unusual pieces of metal-work, pots and planters in every size and shape, sculpture, arbors and arches of wood, metal, and brick, and pretty fences. Lantana, roses, and other woody stemmed plants are pruned into topiary or standard forms. Herbs spill from pots and out of wall crevices. Part of the fun of it all for Mrs. Densmore is making each area flow visually into the next, coordinating textures, colors, and styles.

Mrs. Densmore wrote an article about her garden for the June 1999 issue of *Fine Gardening.* In the article, she emphasizes the importance of defining the parameters of outdoor space using architecture and plants for structure. "It helps to use [materi-

als] that relate to the age and style of your home. Repeating architectural elements of the house . . . also reinforces continuity." She notes that "achieving a balanced sense of scale is essential to creating a harmonious garden room. As with the fences and walls, permanent plants need to be in proper proportion to the objects they're meant to complement."

Today, the garden is a memorial to Mrs. Densmore's husband, Richard, who died in 1996. "Since his death," she writes, " I've gained solace and strength from being in my soul-soothing, outdoor rooms," for her husband also loved his wife's fanciful outdoor creation.

A Garden on Vanderhorst Row

Three symmetrical but entirely different gardens extend behind a significant residence overlooking Charleston's harbor. The handsome brick building, constructed in the oldest section of the city by 1800, is the only survivor of a group of "similar rental complexes, each divided into three three-story town house dwellings," according to Jonathan Poston.

In spite of the location, Hurricane Hugo did little damage to the house in 1989, but the walled-in gardens suffered the storm surge. The Reverend Dr. and Mrs. Frank McClain purchased the southernmost section of the tenement in 1991 and decided to consult Mary Zahl, a local landscape designer, to make some changes to their garden section.

Previous owners had built a six-foot high brick wall along the property line to the north, giving more privacy to the approximately seventy-five-foot long and twenty-five-foot wide garden. A pretty goldfish pond had also been added. Drawings on an early plat showed that a kitchen, privy, and warehouse once existed where the garden

Spires of purple larkspur accentuate the flowerbeds in spring.

FACING PAGE: *The goldfish pond.*

now lies. The outlines of these buildings were evident in the old wall to the south and gave inspiration for Mrs. Zahl's division of the area into three separate garden rooms.

The first room, a paved terrace, has a gated entrance via a 75-foot walkway along the southern facade of the residence. A tall and effective privacy hedge of ligustrum and cherry laurel trees screens the house and walkway from both the sun and nearby commerce. The terrace is usually entered through the house, and the entire garden can be overlooked from a second-story porch facing the harbor to the east. From the terrace, which is furnished with openwork iron chairs, chaises, and tables, the walk narrows between a quartet of conically pruned *Ilex* 'Nellie Stevens' and leads to the middle garden. Here, the centerpiece is the pond, full of bright orange fantail goldfish and surrounded by ferns and potted topiaries. In spring, the Cherokee rose *(Rosa Laevigata)* displays crisp single white blossoms along the wall behind the fountain, mingling with ivy and several other old roses in pastel tints. Opposite the pond is a low knot garden of *Serissa foetida* and a bench. In pleasant weather, the garden is frequently used for entertaining.

Different footing lends much interest to the changes in the succession of "rooms." Flagstones around a rice millstone in the terrace give way to patterned brick in the center garden and finally to a thick St. Augustine grass lawn. Marking the entrance to the third garden is a double-vaulted iron arbor supporting pale pink roses with strawberry begonia, a variegated-leaf groundcover *(Saxifraga stolonifera),* planted underneath. A small maple tree in the corner and a crab apple balance a dogwood at the far end, where an ironwork gate set in an arch in the wall gives an enticing glimpse of water in the distance.

Flowerbeds bordered by brick "soldiers and sailors" (half bricks standing against whole brick pavers next to the grass) surround the lawn and are planted with an assortment of annuals and perennials. Mrs. McClain, an experienced flower arranger who has participated in many seminars and demonstrations, particularly loves working with the plants in this section. To the north, a trio of camellias (an unidentified red, 'Catherine Cathcart,' and 'Debutante') gives a glossy dark green background to spring plantings of maroon and white rocket snapdragons, purple larkspur, an assortment of lavender, white, and pink stock, blue pansies, snowy white alyssum, and pale yellow petunias. A seasonal assortment follows. On the shadier south side, leatherleaf, holly *(Cyrtomium falcatum),* and autumn ferns mix with white azaleas, fatsia, and dwarf gardenias. There are also alstroemerias, blue hydrangeas, and salvias. An enormous *Celtis laevigata* (sugarberry, hackberry, nettle tree), remarkably not blown down by the hurricane, grows just outside the far wall. It lends a soft, airy backdrop of pale green leaves and pale gray branches and also lends an air of maturity to this new garden in an eighteenth-century ruin.

The Garden of the Thomas R. Waring House

Constructed in 1912, this large Colonial Revival townhouse was originally situated on an L-shaped lot. In 1991, the lot was subdivided and Sheila Wertimer, a local landscape architect, installed the structure of the current garden for the woman who was then in residence. The present owners, a family with young children, wanted to increase privacy and simplify the look of the garden.

Mr. and Mrs. Lee were experienced gardeners who appreciated the well-chosen plant material already in place around the small lawn behind the house. The garden is enclosed by six-foot high brick walls, but a major visual problem had to be addressed. A view of the dowdy back of a rambling Victorian house that had been divided into several condominiums could be seen from every window facing south and from the pretty two-storeyed porches gracing the garden facade of the Lee's house. Nine Savannah hollies *(Ilex opaca)* were planted against the walls to form a high evergreen screen and are well on the way to their mature height of thirty to forty feet. Unfortunately, a mature flowering crabapple had to be removed because the local rat population discovered the fruit and exploited the tree's proximity to the upstairs porch.

Masses of pink azaleas were removed. The shrubs had grown to a height and width which covered the rails of the porch leading into the garden. Other azaleas formed a backdrop against the lawn and were replaced with Mrs. G.G. Gerbing, a white-flowering variety. White, which is Mr. Lee's favorite, was also chosen for the camellias espaliered along the driveway. Exotic vining gloriosa lilies *(Gloriosa rothschildiana)* planted at the bases of the camellias produce spectacular crimson flowers rimmed in yellow during the summer and die down before the camellias are ready to bloom in the winter months. White 'Lamarque' roses, which are 1830 Noisettes, cover the wrought iron fence in front of the house and were given as a housewarming gift.

From the back porch, brick steps lead down onto a small stone patio and an airy furnished pergola covered with Confederate jasmine *(Trachelospermum jasminoides)*. The space is further defined by the addition of large pots filled with clipped boxwoods, a feature Mr. Lee especially likes to use. He also enjoys a show of bulbs in the spring and different types of hydrangeas for cool summer bloom. For the Lees, constant pruning is the key to the formal, manicured look they prefer. At night, a carefully designed lighting system softly plays up the topiaries, statuary, and other formal features of the garden, transforming it into a candlelit room outdoors.

FACING PAGE, ABOVE: *The Thomas R. Waring house.*
FACING PAGE, BELOW: *A view of the pergola and background screen plantings of Savannah hollies.*

The Garden of the
Henry Porter Williams House

Built in 1837, the Williams House has been owned by the Geer family since 1900. An imposing white-stuccoed three-storeyed building with triple bay windows, it overlooks Charleston's famous harbor. Although a cotton broker built a large mansion immediately to the south of the Williams House in the 1850s, a narrow strip of property remained between the two houses and served as the garden.

Because of the location, the house and garden were hit particularly hard by Hurricane Hugo in 1989. Seven feet of sea water—full of shrimp, crabs, fish, seaweed, and marsh reeds—inundated the property. The house, which had been raised several feet off the ground in 1903, had three feet of water on the first floor and a badly damaged roof.

But the garden and its main feature, an elegant Victorian children's playhouse, took precedence for immediate repair. The dowager Mrs. Geer was distraught that not only had the little folly built for her in 1903 been flipped over by the high winds, but a neighbor's roof had fallen on top of the jumbled mess. Nearby, on a high ledge behind a pear tree that miraculously escaped damage, Figaro, her cat, refused to leave the perch that had provided shelter during the storm. Other things had to wait until the little house and the cat were rescued.

Betty Geer, wife of the present owner, is a master gardener and longtime proprietor of a flower shop. The relatively clean slate provided by the storm encouraged her to make changes and to be creative in the small space which constituted the entire garden: a narrow strip of lawn beside the house bordered by beds; an open area beyond the back door; and a parking court directly behind the house. Soon, a potting area evolved near the playhouse where she could work on the numerous large planters that decorate the generous porches and soften the edges of the parking area. Several pomegranate (*Punica Granatum*) trees had been destroyed in the loosely defined area at the back of the property near the doll house, where, at the suggestion of one of her sons, she had Charleston Aquatic Nurseries put in a small pond with a bubble fountain.

A rose bed has recently been added along the brick walk next to the house. It had to be raised, which is good for drainage, and was absolutely necessary here because of the high salt water table, which lies about one-and-a-half feet below the lawn. A thick ligustrum hedge gives privacy from the sidewalk and helps deflect some of the

spray from the harbor, but the St. Augustine grass is salt tolerant, as are most of the shrubs and other plants.

An unexpected result from the storm was the sudden appearance of plants whose seeds had been blown in by the wind or deposited with the silt from the storm surge. Mazus, a lovely, delicate groundcover, sprang up between the bricks of the paths. Asiatic jasmine cropped up all over the garden, and a Vitex Agnus-Castus (chaste tree) sprouted horizontally from a wall, about three feet above the ground, where it still thrives.

The multi-storeyed facade of a neighboring house to the west reflects and retains warmth, which helps semi-tropicals flourish. Three tibouchina shrubs, which were dying in huge pots on an upstairs porch, were transplanted down to this protected area, where they have grown to over eight feet and provide a gorgeous display of exotic purple blossoms in the early fall. The parking area, which is adjacent to the tall protecting wall, is dominated in spring by the cascades of a yellow Lady Banksia rose

The Henry Porter Williams house on East Bay Street.

entwined with a white single-flowered Cherokee rose, *Rosa Laevigata.* A flowering peppermint peach tree and an exuberant yellow jasmine add to the display. Fig and pear trees produce enough fruit for several cases of preserves and chutney each year.

One of the most eye-catching features of the property is the row of six window boxes running the length of the northern side of the house, along the street. Mrs. Geer gets so many compliments from friends, neighbors, and visitors about the boxes that she feels an obligation to keep them going all year. "The salt spray, wind, and heat make planting the boxes especially difficult in the summer, but at least they don't get direct sunlight," she explains. "This summer a combination of herbs, hardy ferns, coleus, and sweet potato vines with both chartreuse and burgundy leaves was particularly successful."